JEWELS
OF HEBREWS

By Stephanie Pavlantos

 M Zion Ridge Press LLC

Mt Zion Ridge Press LLC
295 Gum Springs Rd, NW
Georgetown, TN 37366

https://www.mtzionridgepress.com

ISBN 13: 978-1-949564-91-4

Published in the United States of America
Publication Date: December 1, 2020

Editor-In-Chief: Michelle Levigne
Executive Editor: Tamera Lynn Kraft

TABLE OF CONTENTS

DEDICATION

To Marilyn, my mentor and friend. I am so thankful for you and to the Lord for bringing you into my life thirty years ago. You taught me how much Yeshua loves me, and you gave me a love for God's Word.

To Yeshua, my Savior, may this study glorify You!

Introduction

During the summer of 2016, the Lord impressed upon my heart to read the book of Hebrews. Hebrews? *Why Hebrews? Lord, isn't there another book to study?* However, once I read those first few verses, I was smitten. The Lord had me at "exact imprint." When I finished, I felt prompted to reread it. I knew the Lord wanted to teach me as I mined deeply buried treasures within this book. I hope as we dig into it together, you will discover priceless gems to apply to your life, too.

Here is some rich history to set the stage for Hebrews. First, Yeshua is the Aramaic name Messianic Jews use for Jesus. In this study, we will refer to Jesus as they did with the name Yeshua. Aramaic is part of the subfamily of the Semitic languages. Both Daniel and Ezra were written in Aramaic and many Israelites spoke it at the time of Yeshua.[1]

In the years following Yeshua's ascension into heaven, churches formed small groups that met in homes six or seven days a week. Many house churches, some made up of Gentiles, while others included Messianic Jews, also assembled into larger groups at various times. In many places, these little home churches underwent persecution and infiltration by false teachers or prophets (Heb. 13:9).

The writer of Hebrews sent a sermon of encouragement in the form of a letter shared among the Messianic Jewish churches. Scholars do not know the exact date the author wrote the book of Hebrews but assume it was before the fall of Jerusalem in AD 70 since he wrote of the temple, sacrifices, and high priests as if they were still in place. We do not know the church's location or the writer's name. But we suspect the Jews who rejected Yeshua as the Messiah persecuted this audience (10:32-34), causing them to fall into sin (3:12), to give up meeting together (10:23-25), and to return to Judaism, leaving their faith in the Messiah.

Today, we can empathize with those Messianic Jews from Hebrews who faced evil and rejection for their faith in Yeshua because media, college campuses, and businesses criticize Christians and do not tolerate biblical beliefs. It may be acceptable to say "God," but mention the name of Yeshua or Jesus and problems ensue. Satan's ways have not changed. He does not need new methods and tactics, because his ancient ones still work. We must know how to stand against him in faith.

As we begin our quest through the book of Hebrews, ask the Father to grant you wisdom, discernment, and understanding through the Holy Spirit.

Hebrews, although written to the Jewish believer, is a letter that can encourage all saints. Yeshua loves you through your struggles, challenges, and trials. He and His promises have not changed. Second, it is written to caution against falling into unbelief and laziness in studying the Word so we can stand against the schemes of the evil one. Our relationship with the Son of God is of the utmost importance. Yeshua is our beloved treasure, and we are His masterpieces.

Each chapter will represent a different gem, and its color will reflect the meaning in the verses of Scripture. As you read, look for verses that reveal the gemstone's color. You will find the treasure hiding within each chapter and you will uncover the *Jewels of Hebrews*.

Chapter 1 - Amethyst
Royalty, Kingship, and *Majesty*

Day One

King Edward VIII of England abdicated his throne for the love of an American divorcee, Wallis Simpson, in 1936. As King, he could not take her as his bride, so he gave his kingship to his brother, George, and married the woman he adored. They became the Duke and Duchess of Windsor. In 1947, the Duke gave his wife a stunning necklace made with twenty-seven amethysts. The $6 million piece featured a sizeable heart-shaped amethyst accented with diamonds and set in gold. [1]

During the Middle Ages, the amethyst was known as the "Jewel of the Gods." Only royalty owned the scarce jewel. [2] In Hebrew, *amethyst* means *dream stone* because people believed it produced pleasant dreams. [3] The gem's striking, purple color stands for *royalty, kingship,* and *majesty*. [4]

Let's start today by reading **Hebrews 1:1-4**. (We will use the English Standard Version (ESV) in this study.) The fourteen verses in this chapter use many scriptures from the Old Testament (Tanakh) to make a point. I love the rich meaning in the first four verses. While reading these verses, notice the words and pictures created by the writer and find the significance of this jewel.

What strikes you most about these first four verses?

_____

_____

Contrasts are used to show distinctions between two or more groups, individual things, or people. We also use diversity to show change or the difference between right and wrong. When studying the Bible, contrasts help me put people and things into perspective. The first two verses use this technique.

Write the contrasts you see.

_____

_____

These contrasts set up a few themes for this book, which we will see in the upcoming chapters of this study.

Think about how your parents or grandparents used to do things. How often have you heard, "In those days" or "When I was young"? Many things have changed for the better, while others did not.

Consider the library. As a child, we used card catalogs to find books; now everything is digital and takes less time. Today, we can type a word in our computer's search engine and get a list of information instead of researching many books.

Thirteen times in Hebrews, better is used to describe Yeshua's superiority over people and things. What does it mean to be better or superior to something else? In Greek, the word κρείττων or *kreittōn* means "better," and translates into "greater" or "superior." [5]

Humans may be in the animal kingdom as far as the study of science goes, but we are superior to all animals because God gave us higher brain functions and souls. Genesis 1:26 tells us:

Then God said, "Let us make man in our image, after our likeness. And let them have dominion over the fish of the sea and over the birds of the heavens and over the livestock and over all the earth and over every creeping thing that creeps on the earth."

1

Similarly, within the Heavenly realm, Yeshua is superior to us. God said in Isaiah 55:9, *For as the heavens are higher than the earth, so are my ways higher than your ways, and my thoughts than your thoughts.*

This is still significant today because we often forget Yeshua is not just another man or prophet, as false religions would have us believe; He is the Son, Emmanuel—He is God. The writer of Hebrews contrasts the Son of God with the old ways, thereby supporting Yeshua's superiority.

The Prophet

We will study the Torah, or the first five books of the Bible written by Moses, as it relates to Hebrews. A few years ago, I attended a class on the Torah taught by a local messianic rabbi. His thought-provoking teaching made me appreciate how relevant these books are to our understanding of the New Testament and our daily lives. As we explore these books, I hope you experience the same amazement.

But first, let's consider the biblical author's use of descriptive, symbolic language in the form of types and shadows. The Blue Letter Bible (www.blueletterbible.com) says a *type* can be a person, event, or thing which *foreshadows* a future person, event, or thing. It explains *shadows* as an Old Testament type that is not the *real thing* but a revelation of the real thing. [6] When you see your shadow, it is only a representation of your body, not you. We will see in the Old Testament people with messiah-like actions and qualities. They foreshadow, but are not, the Messiah.

Start with **Hebrews 1:1**, and please read **Deuteronomy 18:15-19** and **John 5:42-47**. The authors refer to the same person in both passages.

In Deuteronomy 18:15, whom is God saying the prophet will be like?

_____

In these last days (Heb. 1:2), how has God spoken to us?

_____

Moses was the first prophet God entrusted with His people, and Yeshua was the last and greatest. While on Earth, Yeshua fulfilled His destiny so that He, the perfect prophet, may live within us through the Holy Spirit. His Spirit fulfills the role of prophet by communicating God's will to our hearts, leading us in the ways of God. John 16:13 says:

When the Spirit of truth comes, he will guide you into all the truth, for he will not speak on his own authority, but whatever he hears he will speak, and he will declare to you the things that are to come.

The Holy Spirit can speak to us in many ways. How does He speak to you?

_____

_____

Amethyst - Day Two
Royalty, Kingship, and *Majesty*

The first verse in which the Holy Spirit spoke to me was John 1:29, *Behold, the Lamb of God, who takes away the sin of the world!* He revealed that John (the Baptist) prophesied about Yeshua. It may seem like a no-brainer now, but at the time it was a revelation. I had not seen John in that light before. After that, I looked forward to the Holy Spirit showing me insights I did not "see" in Scripture.

Reading Scripture is more than a ritual to check off our list. It should be an exploration. The Father wants us to experience His Word. Like a treasure map where **X** marks the spot, the Bible is our map to find the hidden secrets of the ✞, which leads us to Yeshua. Imagine God guiding us along His path of love, encouragement, and wisdom every time we open His Word. He is eager to show us His Son's heart, love, and selflessness, so we will treasure Yeshua as God does.

The author of Hebrews highlights seven characteristics and actions of Yeshua that set Him apart from everyone else. Today, we will study the first two in **Hebrews 1:2-3.**

1. He is *the heir of all things* (Heb. 1:2).

What is an heir? Merriam-Webster defines an *heir* as "one who inherits or is entitled to succeed to a hereditary rank, title, or office, *heir to the throne.* [7]" Turn to **Psalm 2:8** and **Daniel 7:13-14.**

What do these two passages state concerning Yeshua's inheritance?

_____

Have you ever inherited something? We often think inheritance means receiving something of value like money, furniture, or land. But we can also inherit good and bad traits from our family, a problem or money pit. Yeshua inherited a kingdom from His Father, a kingdom full of nations and people who will serve Him now and forever. This is the kingdom Yeshua refers to in the Gospels when He teaches on the kingdom of God.

Read **Daniel 7:13-14**. In these verses, the Son of Man is Yeshua, and the Ancient of Days is God the Father.

How is Yeshua's dominion (sovereignty) and kingdom described?

_____

_____

2. *Through whom [God] created the world* (Heb. 1:2)."

Read **John 1:1-3**. How does John refer to Yeshua?

_____

Who is Yeshua with? Who is He said to be?

_____

Verse 3 declares all things were made through Him and nothing was made without Him.

[He] was God, and he was at the beginning with God (John 1:1-2). The Word is both the spoken word and the Word made Flesh (John 1:14).

God spoke and still speaks; His words will never pass away (Matt. 24:35). His Word is power, and

His words are powerful. God spoke and created all things. He spoke by the prophets, and He spoke by His Son. Read the following explanation about God's Name, Elohim. I hope it adds to your understanding of the Trinity and God's Name.

God is referred to as Elohim in Genesis 1--the account of creation. This name for God in the Hebrew language is אֱלֹהִים, and it consists of five consonants (read right to left). Hebrew is both a written and pictorial language. Each letter represents a picture or symbol adding to its meaning. The first letter of Elohim is an Aleph, or א. It illustrates an ox and stands for leader or father. The next consonant, depicted by a shepherd's crook, is a Lamed or ל, and it symbolizes the son or shepherd. The third character is a Hey or ה, and it portrays a man with his arms raised. It represents the Holy Spirit or revealer. The fourth consonant, signifying a mighty deed or life, is a Yod or י, while the last letter is a Mem or מ, and suggests separation of the waters. This name for God is a plural, masculine word, and this one name contains the Father, the Son, and the Holy Spirit pictured as the mighty Creator. [8]

The Father, Son, and Holy Spirit are one, yet separate. They are equal and interdependent upon each other. All three exhibit qualities of the Creator. God may be the Designer, while the Son creates. Like an architect who designs and draws the blueprints and the engineer who builds what he sees on the plans. We never want to say God is "one entity," or has "one characteristic." It's not good to limit any one person of the Godhead by a specific trait or "duty." The Trinity is like a multi-faceted, priceless diamond reflecting each other's beauty. Individually and together, they possess everything good, holy, and perfect.

Amethyst - Day Three
Royalty, Kingship, and Majesty

From Daddy, with Love

At a church I attended for many years, the pastor's wife referred to God as Abba, or Daddy, in her prayers. I loved to hear her pray. While to some it may seem irreverent, saying the word Daddy has a certain intimacy to it. Today's lesson might convince you it is all right to see Him as your daddy.

We have already studied the first two characteristics of Yeshua: **He is** *the heir of all things* and *Through whom [God] created the world* (Heb. 1:2). Today we will look at three, four, and five. Fasten your seat belts!

Start by re-reading **Hebrews 1:1-3**.

3. **He is** *the radiance of the glory of God* **(Heb. 1:3).**

In the Greek, *radiance* means "reflected brightness" as in "Christ perfectly reflects the majesty of God" [9] and the word in Hebrew for *glory* is Sh'khinah which means, "that which dwells," "to dwell," "reside." [10] This phrase can mean "the brightness and the dwelling of God."

According to the Tanakh (Old Testament), no one could see God and live (Ex. 33:20). However, turn to **Exodus 24:9-11**.

Please read and explain it in your own words.

_____

_____

_____

Is it possible they saw Yeshua, not God the Father? Absolutely. Look at the next descriptive phrase:

4. **He is** *the exact imprint of His nature* **(Heb. 1:3).**

The *exact imprint* or *very expression* comes from the Greek word χαρακτήρ, or *charaktēr*, which looks like the English word *character*. [11] Yeshua embodies God's nature. So, what is that character? The book of Psalms tells us many things about God's personality. Please turn to **Psalm 145:13-20**. The ESV includes this sentence before verse 14: *The Lord is faithful in all his words and kind in all his works.*

What else do you see about God's ways and His works in this passage?

_____

_____

What characteristics of God in **Psalm 145** you most need today?

_____

_____

"The exact imprint of His nature" also means, "A mark or figure burned in or stamped on, an impression." [12]

My husband, Mike, built our children a swing set and fort with a slide and tunnel. He started it in our garage in the middle of winter. I have the cutest pictures of my three bundled children sitting on the steps of the garage watching my husband, hammer nails, saw wood and piece together this gift they were eager to play on .

On Father's Day, I gave Mike a small plaque inscribed with "From Daddy, with love" to attach to the wooden beam of the playset so my children would always remember its creator. My kids are nearing the end of their college careers and that playset still stands in our yard.

Yeshua exemplifies this same inscription from our Father in Heaven. God sent His Son as a loving imprint of His nature and love for us. *For God so loved the world that He gave His only Son…* (John 3:16) or you could say, "From Daddy, with love."

5. *He upholds the universe by the word of His power* **(Heb. 1:3).**
Please read **Colossians 1:15-17**. These verses are very much like **Hebrews 1:3**.
Record the similarities.

_____

_____

In all the verses about creation in **Genesis 1:3-26**, each day starts with *God said…* God the Father used His words to design, plan, and set things in motion, and Yeshua spoke to create and to preserve (or uphold) all things. Yeshua is the Creator (John 1: 3), so it makes sense He made us in His image. We do not know God's physical image because He is spirit, but we know Yeshua's by reading the Gospels.

Matthew 24:35 says, *Heaven and earth will pass away, but my words will never pass away.* Notice the verse does not say *The Word* but, *my words.* This verse is not speaking of Yeshua but of *every word* God and Yeshua have articulated!

Amethyst - Day Four
Royalty, Kingship, and *Majesty*

Friendship with God

So far, we have seen Yeshua as the heir of all things, the creator of all things, the radiance of God's glory, the exact imprint of God's nature, and the upholder of the universe with the word of His power. Today, we study the last two characteristics of Yeshua from Hebrews 1. Yeshua restored our relationship with God through His sacrifice. God never wanted us to be separated from Him, but sin is the great alienator.

There have been times in my life when a serious difference of opinion or belief ended a friendship. There have been some incidents where the Lord led me to walk away from the friendship after I forgave them, because that relationship was toxic to my spiritual walk. Other times He directed me to not only forgive but reconcile with that person. There are some relationships God considers too important for us to walk away.

Before starting this section, consider how we can feel when we are aware of disobedience in our lives. Is it hard to pray or feel close to God? Sin disconnects us from Him, just as hard feelings or bitterness divides us from our family or friends. Relationship with Yeshua is about reconciliation with God and others.

I pray these Scriptures change the way you see Him. Read **Hebrews 1**:1-4, again.

6. *He made purification for sins.*

Everything listed in one to five has been about *who* Jesus is, but numbers six and seven are about *what* He does. In his blog, *Thus Said the LORD*, Michael Peterson describes that purification requires four things from a sinner: [13]

1. Confession
2. Repentance
3. Sacrifice
4. Atonement (or Reconciliation)

Yeshua took care of numbers three and four when He made propitiation, or appeasement, for sin. He was the Lamb of God, who took away the sins of the world (John 1:29).

Please read **Romans 5:10-11**. The word *reconciliation*, at the end of verse 11, translates into *atonement*.

What was our condition before Yeshua reconciled us?

_____

_____

If you have a King James Version (KJV), it already uses the word *atonement*, but The New Living Translation (NLT) puts it this way, *For since we were restored to friendship with God by the death of his Son while we were still his enemies...* We were **restored to friendship** (with God) while we were enemies of God.

For most of my life, I believed I needed to be good in order to please God by obeying the rules and doing what my pastor and family told me to do. It was my job to be obedient so God would love me. After college, the Lord put a godly woman in my life. Her name is Marilyn. Through her, I learned Yeshua wanted a relationship with me more than He wanted me to follow rules. He wants to be my friend, my brother, and the lover of my soul. He wants us to want Him more than anything or anyone else, because that is how He feels about us.

Have you considered your relationship with God a friendship and a sonship? How might this knowledge make you see God differently?

_____

_____

According to **Romans 5:10**, what happens once we are reconciled?

_____

The word "saved" is the Greek word *sozo*. It means "to save a suffering one (from perishing), i.e., one suffering from disease, to make well, heal, restore to health." [14]

Yeshua means Salvation. Matthew 1:21 says, *For she will bear a son, and you shall call his name Jesus, for he will save his people from their sins.*

Yeshua rescued us from eternal punishment, sicknesses, emotional pain, and brokenness, and from spiritual death. Yeshua can heal us physically, emotionally, and spiritually. In some cases, it can happen at the time of salvation, or instantly after a prayer for healing, but it is often a journey. We can be healed over time with medical intervention, emotional counseling, or ongoing prayer. When a loved one dies of cancer, a heart attack, or some other disease, healing of their physical bodies happens in Heaven.

There are other reasons we suffer from illness and disease. Spiritual or emotional problems, such as unforgiveness or bitterness can cause physical ailments. [15] Yeshua gave us life and health through His death and suffering.

Yeshua can also save us from strongholds like rejection, control, and fear. I wrestled with rejection. When someone seemed to disregard an idea, thought, or belief I shared, I personally felt disrespected. I believed people were talking about me if I saw or heard whispering. If someone backed out on plans or dropped out of my Bible study, I viewed it as a problem with me. Most of the time none of these things were true, but it seemed so real.

I agreed with the evil one when he whispered in my ear, "They are rejecting you!" After a while, he didn't need to tell me. My mind and emotions jumped to their own conclusions. The Lord healed my feelings of rejection when I repented for believing and agreeing with Satan's lies and replaced them with scripture like **Psalm 139:14**, *I praise you, for I am fearfully and wonderfully made.*

What type of healing do you want or need?

_____

Ask Yeshua to heal you. Make sure to ask others to pray for you in this area as well. Write your prayer below.

_____

_____

_____

Yeshua is the ultimate sacrifice and atonement for our sin, but confession and repentance are our responsibility. We must come to Him in humility, confessing our sin, and turn from lies and wrongdoing and walk in truth (1 John 1:9).

7. *He sat down at the right hand of the Majesty on high* (Heb. 1:3)

According to the *Jewish New Testament Commentary*, the right hand of God is *not a place* but an exalted status the Messiah has as the High Priest of God. [16] Yeshua is serving as our High Priest, like the priests did during the days of the Temple. We will cover this in more depth later.

What does sitting down at the right hand of God make Yeshua?

_____

_____

Verse 4 states that His name (Jesus) is more excellent (or superior) than the angels. This is the first of thirteen times we will see the word "superior" or "better."

How has today's reading changed your view of Yeshua?

_____

_____

_____

Amethyst – Day Five
Royalty, Kingship, and *Majesty*

The Bridegroom

Who did or do you dream of your future husband resembling? Maybe you like the romantic, or maybe you like the strong and silent type. Maybe it's the warrior/military type or the happy-go-lucky type of man; or a combination of more than one? Maybe you are the kind of woman who doesn't see herself married. That's okay, too. But whether we are married in this life or not, we have a Bridegroom waiting to see us face-to-face one day.

Today, the significance of the amethyst color will become more evident. We will examine many Old Testament passages to reveal Yeshua. Although we may not see it, the Messiah is referenced throughout the Bible. I like to cross-reference the New Testament verses and read them in the original context of the Old Testament. I will even comment in my Bible where and how they are used elsewhere.

We will study the difference between Yeshua and the created angels and the importance of Yeshua's position and title.

Read **Hebrews 1:5-14**. Some of these verses come from the Old Testament and have a common thread throughout.

In verse 5, **Psalm 2:7** and **2 Samuel 7:14** are quoted. What idea is repeated in these verses?

_____

Verse 6 states, *When he brings the firstborn into the world...* We use the word *firstborn* to describe the first child born to us. But, in this context, the word *firstborn* means a position of honor and rank.[17] (It was also used to describe Solomon, even though he was the tenth son of David.)

Deuteronomy 32:43 and **Psalm 104:4** are quoted in Hebrews 1:6-7.

What function or purpose do angels have according to these verses?

_____
_____

Skip down to **Hebrews 1:13-14**. What is the angels' purpose in verse 14?

_____

Turn to **Colossians 2:18** and **Galatians 1:8**.

What do these verses have to say about angels?

_____

Both Islam and Mormonism began because of so-called angels giving a revelation other than the Gospel.
Please read **2 Corinthians 11:14**.

So, why does the writer of Hebrews spend so much time trying to convince us that Yeshua is greater than the angels?

Yeshua is Truth. He is the only one we can trust.

Lastly, read **Hebrews 1:8-12**. Verses 8 and 9 come from **Psalm 45:6-7**. Please turn to **Psalm 45** and read the whole Psalm.

Paying special attention to **Psalm 45:10-17**, what is the king getting ready to do?

The Bridegroom has been selected; He has paid the price and has chosen you to be His Bride. The Father alone knows the wedding day, and He has a galaxy-sized marriage feast planned. Now is the time to get to know your Bridegroom. Now is an opportunity to share your heart with your Bridegroom and get to know His heart. Fall in love with Him. You will have all of eternity to spend with Him, but you can start now.

This Psalm is a beautiful picture of Yeshua as the Bridegroom coming for His exquisite bride arrayed in robes interwoven with gold. The bride is told: *Forget your people and your father's house, and the king will desire your beauty. Since he is your lord, bow down to him* (Ps. 45:10-11).

In Luke 14:26 and Matt 10:37, Yeshua told those who wanted to follow Him to leave everything and to love Him more than their mothers, fathers, brothers, and sisters. He wants us to put Him first before all things and all people in our life, even our ministry. He is our King. Let's bow down and seek His presence above anyone else. He deserves it.

Finally, in **Hebrews 1:10-12**, how is Christ described?

Notice in verse 8, the words *forever and ever* are used; in verse 11, the phrase *but you remain;* and in 12, it states, *But you are the same and your years will have no end.* All these verses point to Yeshua as being eternal. He is the Creator who has a plan for all ages and a design for each nation, tribe, and person. He was here before time began and will still be here when it ends.

God started His plan before creation, and you are part of it. He will use you to His glory and praise if you let Him. The Father controls time; He is not hurried or slow. Time will not run out on you, because what He started, He will complete. Amen.

Did you discover the **amethyst**? Where is it in this chapter? In which verses did you uncover royalty, majesty, and kingship?

What did the Holy Spirit reveal and teach you in this chapter?

Who is this King and Bridegroom? He is the heir to all things. He created the world and upholds it by the word of His power. He is the radiance of God's glory and the imprint of His exact nature, and

He is Yeshua, the Son. He is superior to all living things.

As in our story at the beginning of this chapter, we, too, have a King who gave up His throne for love. It wasn't just the love of one woman but all men, women, and children, past, present, and future. He even died for His love. We are His love.

Chapter 2 -Topaz
The divine nature of Yeshua, glory, and *faith*

Day One

A Great Salvation

The Braganza diamond is a topaz weighing 1,680 carats. In the jungles of Portugal, three ex-convicts discovered it in a dried-up riverbed while they were searching for gold to purchase their freedom. With this discovery they believed God answered their prayers. Eventually, the governor and King John VI released them from the jungle, and the topaz became the property of the Royal House of Braganza, from which it derived its name. [1] Some believe topaz derives its name from an ancient Indian word meaning fire, tapas.

The natural, untreated color of topaz is a golden brown to yellow gemstone. It can be blue, pink, and red if irradiated and treated with heat. [2] Its raw color denotes the *divine nature of Yeshua, glory,* and *faith*. [3]

A jewel's hardness is rated from one to ten on a Mohs scale.[4] This scale represents how easily a gem can scratch. The topaz is rated an eight, and diamonds are a ten. If a diamond is hit too hard by another diamond, it splits in two. If hit too hard by a diamond or sapphire, topaz will split in two, so this stone requires care.

The Messianic Jews, who received this letter we call the Book of Hebrews, resembled this gem. Hit hard by the Jews, the Jewish people in Hebrews suffered hardship for turning away from a life of legalism to freedom in the Messiah, until broken by persecution. They needed care. The author encouraged them to remain faithful and cautioned them against drifting away and neglecting their salvation because of their difficult circumstances.

They needed to hear it then, and we need to understand today, the Savior we serve is mighty and eternal, high above angels and man, ruling and upholding the universe, and is the Creator and Son of God. He is not a man wanting to be king, He is THE King. We need Him, and He wants us. The King of the Universe passionately delights in you and wants your love!

This is why **Hebrews 2:1** starts with the word, *Therefore.*

Please read **Hebrews 2:1-4**. In the first verse, we read the first of five exhortations or appeals. What is the first appeal?

_____

What is the outcome if we don't do what the writer is admonishing us to do?

_____

_____

So, what is it we have heard? _____

The phrase *drifts away* implies an unanchored boat floating away in a current of water. Ephesians 4:11-15 uses a similar analogy.

Please read **Ephesians 4:11-15** and describe what keeps us from being "tossed back and forth by the waves and carried away by every wind of doctrine..."

Hebrews 2:2 states, *The message declared by angels proved to be reliable.* Turn to **Acts 7:53** and **Galatians 3:19**.

What is the message, and who gave it?

According to the Law, disobedience required punishment, and the punishment fit the level of defiance. No one escaped punishment under the Law. We are all guilty. **Ephesians 2:1-3** says:

And you were dead in the trespasses and sins in which you once walked, following the course of this world, following the prince of the power of the air, the spirit is now at work in the sons of disobedience – among whom we all once lived in the passions of our flesh, carrying out the desires of the body and the mind, and were by nature children of wrath, like the rest of mankind.

This author asks his people how they are to escape the same punishment if they neglect such a great salvation (or what they have heard). In my twenty-seven years of marriage, I participated in Bible studies with many people in which I failed to see growth. The Christian life can be all about us and what we study, learn, or do. We can forget about the One who made us and gave us life. We can neglect the One who wants to spend time with us. Church, worship, tithing, and even Bible study can be motions we go through because they are expected. We can get so caught up in the *doing*, that we are not *being* who God wants us to be. We forget it is all about Yeshua.

He is the Author of our salvation and He is truth. When we feel depleted, we know it is Yeshua who fills us. But if we neglect spending time in prayer and God's Word, our lack of attention will break off our anchor, causing us to drift until intimacy with God disappears.

Together, let's follow Paul's letter to Ephesus. Let's be intentional, spending time with our Father and forgiving others as He forgave us.

And do not grieve the Holy Spirit of God, by whom you were sealed for the day of redemption. Let all bitterness and wrath and anger and clamor and slander be put away from you, along with all malice. Be kind to one another, tenderhearted, forgiving one another, as God in Christ forgave you (Eph. 4:30-32).

Yeshua wants us to seek healing for our hearts and souls. Restoration begins with Yeshua and spreads to every other relationship we have.

Whom do you need to forgive? Are you willing to do it out of obedience to the Lord?

Write the names of those you need to forgive and commit them to prayer. Ask the Lord to help you forgive him or her and then ask Yeshua to heal your heart from the hurt they caused you.

Now, pray for them. Bless them too. You will be free from the hold the enemy has over you.

Topaz - Day Two
The divine nature of Yeshua, glory, and faith

A little lower

Unbalanced doctrine can toss us back and forth, placing more importance on Old Testament laws than on loving the Father, Son, Holy Spirit, and people. We are easily divided over opinions. Different denominations have distinct views of Bible doctrine.

Because legalism lacks love, Yeshua hated its influence over His people. The author recognized some Messianic Jews considered returning to legalism because of persecution, and that was why he wrote the *Letter to the Hebrews.*

For today's lesson re-read **Hebrews 2:1-3**, then we will start with **Hebrews 2:3-4**.

What did the Lord declare and confirm by those who heard?

_____

How did God bear witness to salvation?

_____

_____

Yeshua came to do away with punishment.

1 John 4:18 says, *There is no fear in love, perfect love casts out fear. For fear has to do with punishment, and whoever fears has not been perfected in love.* Fear can cause legalism because it can base God's love on works and twist His love into a series of rules meant to be kept for fear of punishment. We obey God because we LOVE Him, not out of fear of punishment.

God has never tolerated legalism; it will not save us. The Apostle Paul called the Galatians foolish for reverting back to works. Galatians 2:16 says, *Yet we know that a person is not justified (saved) by works of the law but through faith in Christ Jesus....*

Describe an area in your life controlled by fear. God does not want us to be slaves to fear. Ask the Lord to strengthen your faith and remove fear.

Let Yeshua take the fear away so you can be free.

_____

_____

_____

Hebrews 2:4 explains God's signs, wonders, miracles, and gifts of the Holy Spirit to prove Salvation came from Him. Do not resist these excellent gifts or limit God or His Holy Spirit from working in your heart.

Let's move on to **Hebrews 2:5-18**. The writer refers to Psalm 8:4-6.

In verse 7, it says the Son of Man was made, for a little while, lower than the angels. In the first chapter, we discussed how the writer showed us that Yeshua is above angels, but now we read God made Him lower than the angels.

According to **Hebrews 2:7-9**, for what purpose was He made lower than the angels?

_____

_____

If we were to turn back to the Old Testament and read Psalm 8, we might think it is only referring to mankind in the Garden when God gave him dominion over the Earth. However, if we understand it in the context that the "son of man" is the Son of God, we can't help but see it as a prophecy concerning Yeshua. In verses 8 and 9, the writer expounded on the last few lines of this Psalm. This is how the New Living Translation (NLT) states **Hebrews 2:8-9**:

> *8b Now when it says, 'all things,' it means nothing is left out. But we have not yet seen all of this happen. 9 What we do see is Jesus, who 'for a little while was made lower than the angels' and now is 'crowned with glory and honor' because he suffered death for us. Yes, by God's grace, Jesus tasted death for everyone in the entire world.* (The word *tasted*, is the Greek word meaning *experienced*.)

For whom did Yeshua die? For whom did He suffer? For whom did He become lower than the angels? _____

God did not leave anyone out. The Greek word used in **Hebrews 2:9** is the same word used for "whosoever" in **John 3:16**. It means ALL people.

Topaz – Day Three
The divine nature of Yeshua, glory, and faith

How do You see Yeshua?

My dog, Sophie, is mostly outside in our four acres of fenced property with our other animals. She has the most expressive eyes. When she spots me through the window, her ears flap back, and she stares with so much love. Sophie's emotional response is a result of knowing me as someone who loves and cares for her, a person she trusts.

We also measure people according to how they make us feel or what they do for us. We tend to see them through the lens of pain or happiness. In today's lesson, we will explore how we see Yeshua or, maybe, how we should see our Savior.

Read **Hebrews 2:1-9**.
How does verse 9 begin in your version of the Bible? Read this verse in multiple versions if you can.

Record the first four words of verse 9.

_____

Stop and think about these four words.
How do you see Yeshua? Be honest.

_____
_____
_____
_____

Does He laugh? Is He happy? Is He full of joy? Do you see Him with eyes of love? Do you see Him looking at you with disappointment or condemnation? If it's the latter, why do you see Him this way?

_____
_____

Life is hard, right? Do you blame Him, or rely on Him to get you through it?
Sometimes we see Yeshua through our wounded hearts. Hurt, betrayal, and brokenness sometimes skew our perception of Him. Child of God, ask Him to take your pain and brokenness and make you whole. He. Will. Do. It. Healing your broken heart is something Yeshua does so well! You only have to ask. Please, hear me. Yeshua adores YOU. He delights in you, and He is always with you, loving you more than life itself.

Ask Him to show His feelings for you. Write what He shows you.

_____
_____
_____
_____

Sometimes we can overlook the little ways in which He shows us His love. One day, I asked the Lord, "How do I miss the ways You show Your love for me?" But He didn't answer me right away.
As I went outside to feed the dogs, Sophie came running, giving me one of her "looks." At that

moment, Yeshua answered my question. *I look at you the way Sophie looks at you. I love you more than she does.* My eyes filled with tears as His words penetrated my thoughts and heart.

He looks at you with those same eyes of love!

But we see Jesus....

According to **Hebrews 2:9**, how should we see Yeshua now?

_____

_____

What's the reason we see Him like this now as opposed to how we saw Him in the Gospels?

_____

Turn to **Revelation 1:12-18**. In verses 12-16, we "see" Yeshua as He is now. Revelation shows us a depiction of the Messiah we will worship in Heaven for eternity. In verse 18, consider how He describes Himself.

What do you think or feel as you read this description of Yeshua?

_____

_____

_____

God's desire and mine is that you see Yeshua differently than you did before you started this chapter. He is worthy of all praise and honor. Take time to finish this chapter with prayer. Tell Yeshua how you feel about Him, no matter how you feel. Confess anything you must and ask Him to help your view of Him be grounded in truth.

_____

_____

_____

Topaz – Day Four
The divine nature of Yeshua, glory, *and* faith

Crowned with Glory and Honor

Have you ever wanted recognition and fame? There were times I thought I wrote something great on my blog, only to have it barely noticed on social media. The Lord impressed me with a thought, *Who do you want to please, Me or your readers?* That changed my attitude. I repented for putting affirmation from people above God.

I may never have anyone outside my family and community know my name, but God does. Jeremiah 1:5 states, *Before I formed you in the womb, I knew you…* That is the best thing ever! He is the One who matters most.

For today's lesson, we will continue with **Hebrews 2:9** and find out the price paid for glory and honor.

Hebrews 2:9 says, he was *crowned with glory and honor…*
Have you ever thought about the meaning of glory? How would you describe "glory" to someone else?

_____

_____

In the New Testament, the Greek work for *glory* means "splendor, brightness, shining, and radiance." [5] The computer search engine, Google, describes glory as "high renown or honor won by notable achievements." It means fame and prestige. God crowned Yeshua with splendor, fame, and renown when He took our place, suffered, and died. Consider how He came into this world, isn't it proper He should exit it with fame and high renown? That is why I love those verses in **Revelation 1:12-18**. It shows Yeshua as He is. *A King!*

Please consider another phrase in verse 9 we often overlook.

Why did Yeshua need to "taste death?"

_____

_____

God showed His grace to us by letting One die for all. Who could give their child to die for someone we consider extraordinary, let alone someone who is miserably sinful? Only God. He knew we could never be good enough to go to Heaven on our merit or be able to earn righteousness. Because of God's grace and love for us before time began, He provided a way for us to *become the righteousness of God* (2 Corinthians 5:21) through His Son, our Messiah.

Please read **Hebrews 2:10-13**. First, let's distinguish whom the author portrays in these verses. You may already know, but I find it helps to understand the verses better.

Who is "he" in *for whom and by whom all things exist…?*

_____

The Founder (Author or Captain) of Salvation is He who sanctifies (verse 11), or Yeshua.
Let's look at a few other words. The author used the word glory again, but not to describe Yeshua.

Who is brought (or led) to glory, and who does it?

_____

Perfect is the second most used word in Hebrews. In this verse, who is perfected, how is that done, and who does it?

_____

How is God perfecting you? Do you or others see a difference in you or your life over the last few years?

_____
_____
_____

What ways has God used to perfect you?

_____
_____

In a few more verses, we will see why God perfected Yeshua, but let's look again at the word *glory*, which means *splendor, fame, high renown, and good opinion*. No matter what you have heard, what someone told you, or even what you think about yourself, God made you famous in Heaven because of Yeshua. Maybe you don't feel celebrated or well understood, but that is a lie. All of Heaven knows your name. You are famous in your Father's eyes.

God rejected and cast Satan out of Heaven because of his pride, arrogance, and desire to take his Creator's place. Therefore, Satan will do anything to make you feel rejected. John 10:10 tells us, "The thief comes only to steal, kill, and destroy. I came that they may have life and have it abundantly."

In what ways do you experience or feel rejection?

_____
_____

God has not rejected you. It is a place which Satan wants you to live, not God. Rejection keeps us in bondage and affects many areas of our lives. I know this because I struggled with it for so long. My healing came in stages, not all at once. Like an onion, the Lord removes and heals layers of pain, rejection, fear, and other strongholds. People may have rejected you, but you do not have to let it identify you. You are God's child. Repent for believing the lie and tell Satan you will not cooperate with him anymore.

If you still need persuading, here are other verses. Turn to **Ephesians 1:3-6**.

Look at the words Paul uses. He CHOSE us in him BEFORE the foundation of the world... In LOVE, he predestined us for adoption as sons through Jesus Christ...

Read **Ephesians 2:4**. Paul says, *But God, being RICH in mercy, because of the GREAT love with which he loved us EVEN when we were dead in our trespasses...* (Emphasis mine). Does it sound like God has rejected you? Do you believe what God says in these verses? Rebuke Satan's lies and walk in the truth that God dearly loves and accepts you.

In **Hebrews 2:11**, it says, *He who sanctifies and those who are sanctified all have one source, (or are all one).* This is the first of many times we will read about sanctification or consecration. It means "to dedicate, to service and loyalty to God, make holy, sanctify, to cause one to have the quality of holiness."[6]

Who or what is the source of sanctification? _____

As a result, what does Yeshua call us? _____

He is not ashamed... We will see this phrase again later in this study, but does this statement give you joy? Yeshua is NOT ashamed of you. He calls you daughter or son and friend. No matter what you think of yourself or what you may be ashamed of, He is not embarrassed of you. The King of the universe calls you family.

How does that make you feel? Write your prayer of thanksgiving.

_____
_____
_____

Topaz – Day Five
The divine nature of Yeshua, glory, and *faith*

Made like us, so He could help us

A woman from church once told me she believed God would do whatever it takes to make sure we go to heaven; even if it means taking us home "early" to avoid us turning from Him. I have to say that I have never thought of it that way. That perspective can't be proven in Scripture, but I do know God is compassionate. He wants to save us, deliver us, heal us, and help us in every way, even if we don't understand His process. Because His ways and thoughts are higher than ours, what makes sense to Him can confuse us.

We have to trust God knows best and has our best in mind. His love for us is impossible to understand.

Read **Hebrews 2:14-18**.
In verse 14, who are the *children*? In addition, who is the *he*, whom the author mentions?

_____

What did Yeshua share in?

_____

Why? _____

The word for *destroy* in the original Greek means "to put an end to, cause to come to an end, put a stop to, cause to cease to happen." [7]

Whom does Yeshua disarm by His death?

_____

Also, please read **Colossians 2:13-15**. Verse 15 is very similar to **Hebrews 2:14**. The word "disarmed" is a different Greek word in Colossians than in Hebrews. It means "to put off, separate from, or strip off." [8]

Who is disarmed in **Hebrews 2:14** and **Colossians 2:15**?

_____

I love how Paul says, *... put them to open shame, by triumphing over them in it [the cross]* (Col. 2:15). Yeshua not only stripped them of their power but shamed them by His death on the cross. The very cross meant to shame Yeshua humiliated Satan, his principalities, and demons.

God became a man (Yeshua), with flesh and blood like His children, so He could die. He did not die a natural death, but He suffered excruciating pain, so that through His death, burial, and resurrection He could become the Author of our Salvation to eliminate the author of our death.

Read **Hebrews 2:15**.

What does the fear of death lead to?

_____

What will Yeshua do to those enslaved? _____

It is for freedom Christ has set us free (**Gal. 5:1**). Freedom is only found in Christ because we can never attain it on our own. Yeshua is the only deliverer.

Are you experiencing freedom? Why? Why not?

_____

_____

Hebrews 2:9, 14 refer to the death from which Yeshua saves us. Verse 16 says, *For it is not angels he helps, but he helps the offspring of Abraham.* Angels do not die, so He came to keep us from spiritual death. However, everyone physically dies.

Please read **Revelation 2:11**. Yeshua says the conqueror will not see the second death.
Turn to **Revelation 20:14**.

What is the second death?

_____

Yeshua's death saves and continues to heal and restore us from many things in this life and the next.

Please read **Hebrews 2:17-18**.

Why was it so important for Yeshua to be like us in every respect?

_____

_____

In the Old Testament, the high priest served the Lord by making the animal sacrifices for himself, and the nation of Israel. Only the high priest entered the Holy of Holies once a year on Yom Kippur and offered the sacrifice on the Mercy Seat (which sits on the Ark of the Covenant) to atone for his people. This high priest had to have love and compassion for the people he interceded for.

According to **Hebrews 2:17**, why did Yeshua have to be made like us?

_____

Now we will see why Yeshua was perfected (from verse 10).

Please read **Hebrews 2:18**. Why did Yeshua suffer?

_____

Yeshua had to be made like us so He could be a merciful and faithful high priest. Who can understand us any better than one who came in flesh and blood, was tempted, suffered, and died? He *wants to help us* through our temptations, too.

What other god can make these claims? Which other god wants to rescue? What other god loves his people? Which god would come from his magnificent dwelling to be like those he made? Who would consider dying for pitiful, lowly sinners? Only the One True God, the Righteous One who is Faithful and True, who died and is alive forevermore—Yeshua!

No other god in history treats His people like our God. The gods the pagans worshipped in the

Old Testament required their servants cut themselves and sacrifice their children or themselves, and this was done for gods who did not care for them. Not one of those gods would have suffered and died for any of their worshippers.

Did you find how the golden hue of topaz interwove itself into this chapter? His divine nature and glory are for us to experience, not just read about. He is so much more than we can ever imagine. There is more to Scripture than our imaginations can comprehend.

A relationship with Yeshua and the Holy Spirit working together in Word and prayer gives us a better picture of who He is. This understanding will fill your heart with love and admiration for your Savior. Like the Braganza diamond, which got its name from royalty, we derive our name from Yeshua because He pardoned us with His blood. He is our treasure. Seek Him.

Please record anything the Lord showed or spoke to you from this chapter. Did He reveal anything new about Himself or who you are to Him?

_____

_____

_____

_____

Chapter 3 - Emerald
Life, growth, fresh, and *flourishing*

Day One

Everything we need

The Vladimir Tiara is a gorgeous diadem with fifteen intertwined, diamond-encrusted circles, each with a hanging pearl, held together with a diamond ribbon on top. The tiara belonged to the Grand Duchess Vladimir of Russia, who left the diadem in a vault when she fled St. Petersburg in 1918. Her friends smuggled it out of Russia and returned the crown to her before her death in 1920. Her daughter, Princess Nicholas of Greece, sold the damaged tiara to Queen Mary of England. She had it repaired and added fifteen exquisite hanging emeralds to interchange with the hanging pearls. Queen Mary left it to her granddaughter, Queen Elizabeth II. Royal women, from Queen Elizabeth to Princess Diana and Catherine to the Duchess of Cambridge, have worn this incredible tiara. [1]

The Egyptians mined the first emeralds near the Red Sea, and Cleopatra was a big fan of the stone.[2] When visiting dignitaries left Egypt, Cleopatra gifted them with a large emerald with her likeness etched on it. [3]

A brilliant green jewel resembling the greenest of trees, the emerald color means *life, growth, fresh,* and *flourishing.*[4] It is one of the few gems where flaws are a good thing.[5] The inclusions found in emeralds add to their character and uniqueness just as our imperfections add to ours. Scripture mentions emeralds several times; Revelation 4:3 describes a rainbow resembling an emerald around the throne of God.

Before starting Hebrews 3, the Lord had me read the book of Exodus. I didn't realize why until I studied and wrote this chapter. There are key passages the Lord pointed out as He revealed truths about Moses I hadn't seen. I want to share them with you.

Before we start Hebrews 3, let me summarize portions of Moses' story. (If you haven't read this story, you can find it in Exodus chapters 1-14).

Moses was an ordinary man set apart by God when he was a just a baby. But a fearful Pharaoh wanted to kill Hebrew toddlers under the age of two because the Hebrews were having babies like crazy and their population was out of control. If they realized their strength, they might have turned on Egypt and overtaken them. A certain Levite woman, who had two children, put her youngest baby boy in a basket and sent him floating down the Nile. His older sister followed the basket and saw Pharaoh's daughter find her brother and take him as her son. He grew up in the palace. When he found out he was a Hebrew, he became frustrated by the slavery of his people. The Egyptians forced him to leave after he killed an Egyptian man who was beating a slave. Moses fled Egypt and settled in Midian, where he married and had two sons. God met him on a mountain in the form of a burning bush, and He laid out His plan for Moses to rescue the Hebrew people from slavery. Moses felt unqualified at first because he claimed he did not speak well. God relented and let his brother Aaron speak for him.

The two of them spoke to Pharaoh and requested he allow the children of Israel to hold a feast for their God. Pharaoh said, "No," and they repeated this cycle many, many times.

Please read **Exodus 6:1-9**. Highlight or underline every time you read, *I am the LORD*. The word LORD, in capital letters, represents the name *Jehovah, Yahweh,* or *I AM* (a name the Jewish people will not speak because of its holiness).

In her book, *To Know Him by Name*, Kay Arthur wrote:
God is saying, "I am that I am. I am the self-existent one. I am everything and everything you will ever

need." God was saying to his servant, "I am the same one who appeared to Abraham, Isaac, and Jacob and made My covenant with them. Now I am revealing Myself as the One who keeps His covenants! I am about to deliver My people according to My word." [6]

Do you see God this way? Is He Jehovah to you? Is He everything, and everything you will ever need?

_____

_____

Imagine the LORD who fills the universe, looking throughout His creation to find you so He can be everything you need. The next time you cry out to Jehovah for anything, remember these words.

In **Exodus 6:1-9**, by what name did God tell Moses that Abraham, Isaac, and Jacob knew Him?

_____

God's relationship with Moses and the children of Israel would be different. Instead of El Shaddai (God Almighty or All-sufficient One), He was known as the LORD or Jehovah. This name shows He is all-powerful, all-knowing, and eternal. He will show His power to everyone.

In **Exodus 6:7**, we see the phrase, *I will take you to be my people...* Does it remind you of a common ceremony? What ceremony?

_____

I believe this is the first time we see God as the Bridegroom. As a man takes a bride to be his wife for as long as they both live, God was making Israel His bride and would be their LORD forever. Let's look at a different relationship found in Exodus 7.

Please turn to **Exodus 7:1-2**. What relationship is God mirroring between Moses and Aaron?

_____

This verse shows how God deals with us in unique and individual ways. He did not treat Moses the same way He treated Abraham, Isaac, or Jacob. God will not deal with or use us in the same way He does others. I learned this when I wanted to teach and write like Beth Moore. Most of all, I wanted God to use me the way He uses her. But God already has a Beth Moore, and He did not need me to be like her. He needs me to be who He designed me to be.

Have you ever felt this way? Take the time to thank God for your gifts, talents, and uniqueness. Give God permission to use you as He sees fit.

_____

_____

_____

Now, please read **Numbers 12:6-9**. God speaks to Aaron and Miriam, Moses' siblings. God shows He deals with and speaks with Moses differently than with other prophets.

How does God describe Moses in verse 7?

_____

Return to **Numbers 12:3**. How is Moses described by God?

How does God speak with him?

How does the Lord speak to you?

Moses' humility, faithfulness, and servant's heart allowed him to speak openly, as God's friend (**Ex. 33:11**), and God defended him against his family. Moses had one of the most critical jobs in the Old Testament. He led Israel out of Egypt and interceded for them many times to keep the Lord from destroying them. As a prophet and judge, he received, recorded, and instituted the entire Torah, including the Ten Commandments, instructions for the Tabernacle, Ark of the Covenant, and high priest duties, and instructions for the Sabbath and Feasts of the Lord; plus, he mentored Joshua and Caleb to lead the next generation into Canaan. It was an amazing accomplishment. No wonder the Jews, then and today, have a high regard for Moses.

Emerald – Day Two
Life, growth, fresh, and *flourishing*

Moses, a type and shadow of Yeshua

Have you ever witnessed a miracle? Today, we are going to see a few wonders Yeshua performed before many eyewitnesses. Yeshua is still in the business of miracles. Do you ever wonder why we don't see more?

Hebrews 3:1, tells us to *consider Yeshua…* Let's do that. We will turn to John 6 to see how Yeshua was superior to Moses. Read **John 5:45** through **6:14**. In John 5:46, Yeshua says, *[Moses] wrote of me,* which comes from **Deuteronomy 18:15**.

In John 6, what feast is taking place? _____

Timing is everything. Yeshua performs these miracles around important feasts and significant Jewish history. You may or may not be familiar with these miracles, but the first one of this passage is when Yeshua feeds the 5,000 men with two fish and five loaves of bread (John 6:1-15). This whole chapter symbolizes what Moses (through God) did in the *wilderness.*

How does this miracle reflect what Moses did?
_____
_____

How did the people respond in John 6:14?
_____

How does the miracle of Yeshua walking on the water in **John 6:16-21** parallel how Moses parted the Red Sea in Exodus 14:15-18? *Pay special attention to John 6:21.*
_____
_____

The New Testament towns of Capernaum and Tiberias, among others, border the Sea of Galilee. The sea is thirteen miles long and eight miles wide.

How far out had the disciples rowed before they saw Yeshua? What happens next?
_____
_____

Do you see the double miracle in **John 6:16-21**? Explain.
_____
_____

In **John 6:22-59**, many people Yeshua fed with the five loaves and two fish followed Him to Capernaum, and He explained His identity to them.
Read these verses, but pay attention to **John 6:30-36**. Make a note of who they believe gave the manna to their fathers.

How does Yeshua distinguish Himself from the manna?

_____

_____

I love John 6:33 because Yeshua defines the Hebrew word *manna*. Manna is written מן in Hebrew. Reading right to left, the first letter is *mem* מ, and means *to come down from heaven*, like water or dew. The second character is *nun* ן, (pronounced noon) and it signifies *life* or *fish*. [7]

In **John 6:33**, how does Yeshua describe the bread of God?

_____

_____

Everything God did for the Israelites at the time of Moses was to foreshadow Yeshua. What God did through Moses pointed to the One who would lead the whole earth out of captivity and bondage. Moses even prophesied about Yeshua, as we read in Chapter 1.

Millions of people celebrate the Passover meal each year and do not realize how it points to Yeshua as the Messiah. Just as Moses performed signs and wonders for Pharaoh and the children of Israel, how much more did Yeshua do signs and wonders as the Son of God, showing His superiority? Some Jewish people still put Moses on a pedestal, refusing to see Yeshua as their Messiah.

John 6:29-47 uses the word *believe* six times (in the ESV).

There was a time in my life when I had trouble believing Yeshua wanted my best. I was disappointed with God and felt He had let me down. It was a difficult time, and I felt alone. What helped me most was confessing my disappointment to God and to a good friend and prayer. God understands our crises and even our doubts. He doesn't want us to stay in that place.

Read **John 6:41-43** again and compare it with **Exodus 16:6-12**. What are the people doing? Why?

_____

_____

Do you ever find yourself like the people in Exodus? Sometimes making a gratitude list can stop our grumbling. Take time to record what you are thankful for.

Philippians 4:8 tells us, *Finally, brothers, whatever is true, whatever is honorable, whatever is just, whatever is pure, whatever is lovely, whatever is commendable, if there is any excellence, if there is anything worthy of praise, think about these things.*

_____

_____

In the conversation between Yeshua and the people of Israel, Yeshua uses the words *life* and *eternal life* many times. This is an essential concept we will continue to unpack as we read Hebrews 3 and 4. Please read **Hebrews 3:1-2**.

The first word the author uses is *Therefore...* To what is this word referring?

_____

_____

Next, record how he describes the people he's addressing.

What do they, and we, as well, share in?

How does he describe Yeshua?

Another first: Yeshua is called an apostle. It is the Greek word *apostolos,* and it means, "A delegate, a messenger, one sent forth with orders, or one sent with a *commission.*" [8] We read this word multiple times in John. Turn to **John 3:17, 6:29 and 57,** and **John 7:29.** We read in these verses God sent (apostolos) Yeshua. Before His return to heaven, Yeshua sent His disciples on a *Great Commission.* Mathew 28:19 says, *Go therefore and make disciples of all nations, baptizing them in the name of the Father and of the Son and of the Holy Spirit.*

Just as Yeshua died for us, many of His followers have given their lives for their Savior to spread the good news of the Way, the Truth, and the Life.

How is the Great Commission being fulfilled today? How do you think you are fulfilling the Great Commission?

Emerald – Day Three
Life, growth, fresh, and *flourishing*

The Builder

When we first moved into our current house, we had been married for three years. It was everything we wanted in a home. We had an "in-law" suite, a big kitchen, and a master bath. We had no children yet, but we had more than enough room for our future children to play.

We bought it from the original builder, who had only lived in it for two years. After the first couple of major rainstorms, we found wet carpeting in our basement. The builder had not backfilled the block wall with gravel, so the wet clay soaked through the walls of the basement, leading to some flooding. My husband dug around the foundation of the house and filled it in with gravel so water would drain away from the house. For our homes and our lives, it is important to have a builder who knows what he is doing.

In today's lesson, we will see how God is our Master Builder and has an original design for each of us. Let's read **Hebrews 3:2.**

How are Yeshua and Moses similar?

_____

If you recall, part of this verse comes from **Numbers 12:7**, which we read earlier. However, in Numbers 12, God said of Moses, *He was faithful in all my house.* The word *house* here relates to God's people, not a physical home or temple.

Please read **Hebrews 3:3-4.** In this verse, why is Yeshua worthy of more glory than Moses?

_____

_____

Yeshua is the builder. The word *builder* means, "to furnish, equip, prepare, make ready."[9] He knew and planned which parent you would resemble, your personality traits, your passions, dislikes, strengths, and limitations. Our relationships, experiences, environment, pain, and trauma help shape us. Sometimes life makes us into someone God never intended. Make sure it is Yeshua doing the building in your life.

Verse 4 states, *Every house is built by someone, but the builder of everything is God.* We agree the Godhead is the Builder and Creator of everything. However, this verse implies someone, or something, can build upon us. (These verses are talking about people, not structures.)

Who or what has built you? Can you name a few people or events?

_____

_____

Let Yeshua build, equip, and prepare you. Look at what you have written and forgive anyone who has built something ungodly on the foundation God started. Next, ask the Lord to remove every "brick" the other builders used to construct something different from what God started.

Ask Him to reveal how He designed you from your conception. What are the strengths, talents, and personality traits He gave you in your mother's womb? Listen. What is the Holy Spirit telling you? Write the words or pictures He offers you. Images are powerful when God gives them. You need to know the Lord speaks; we don't always take the time to pay attention. *Please understand God neither condemns nor calls you any derogatory name, you are His loved one.*

Write the words or pictures God reveals to you.

_____

_____

_____

_____

Please read **Hebrews 3:5-6**. How are Yeshua and Moses different according to these verses?

_____

_____

The Greek word for *a servant*, to describe Moses in this verse, is not your usual word used for a *servant* in the rest of the New Testament. Scripture uses this word once to describe Moses in verse 5. According to *The Bible Exposition Commentary*, it means, "a voluntary servant who acts because of affection."[10] What Moses did, he did because of his love for God. He may not have started out that way, but I think the more time he spent in God's presence, the more in love he became with his Creator. We can apply this truth to our lives.

The more time you spend in God's presence, the more you will fall in love with Him. God uses those who spend time with Him, who want to know Him better, love Him more, and surrender all they have to Him.

In **Hebrews 3:5-6**, what makes us Yeshua's house?

_____

_____

The Greek word for *hold fast* denotes intensity.[11] It is holding on to something as if not to let it get away. *Confidence* means courage, boldness, confidence, frankness.[12] B*oasting* is rejoicing or glorifying in something.[13]

That something is our Hope. Our hope is Yeshua!

Emerald – Day Four
Life, growth, fresh, and *flourishing*

Heart issues

A friend had an irregular heartbeat that worried her because she could feel her heart beating hard within her chest all day, and it kept her from sleeping, too. We prayed over the phone, and I asked God to heal her heart. Shortly after that, she called to tell me the Lord had healed her.

Within two months, the irregular heartbeat was back. As we prayed again, I felt the Lord impress me with the words, "Her heart problem is a heart problem." There was a spiritual heart problem causing her physical heart to suffer. I told her what I felt. She prayed later about it and told me several weeks later the problem with her heart was gone.

The Lord revealed to her she was holding something against a family member, which caused her to become bitter. After repenting of her resentment, the Lord healed her heart spiritually and physically.

Dealing with our heart issues is a hard subject, but we need to know that Yeshua loves us and wants to help us grow in our relationship with Him. He does not want us to feel condemned but free.

Read **Hebrews 3:7-11.** It quotes Psalm 95:7-11. This passage is the second appeal of the book of Hebrews. The first one was in Hebrews 2:1.

In your own words, write what these verses describe.

_____

_____

_____

Verses 8 and 10 tell us one problem the children of Israel had was a heart issue. What do these two verses say about their hearts?

_____

_____

In **John 12:36-40** there is a similar situation, but instead of the children of Israel and God, this is between Yeshua and the Israelites, or Judeans of His time. Please read these verses and note verse 37.

Now read **Hebrews 3:12.** What is the heart issue here?

_____

What does it lead to in John 12:37?

_____

Finish reading Hebrews 3. The author asks a series of questions and then answers each of them. In verse 19, he leads us to the absolute, main reason a whole generation of people died in the wilderness instead of entering the Promised Land.

What was it?

_____

Several times the author uses the word *today.* He is reminding his audience to remember Moses and the children of Israel.

How does the author refer to the time of Moses and his people in verses 8 and 15?

_____

Now, think about everything you read, and the questions asked regarding verses 12-19. We have talked about the *heart, unbelief,* and *rebellion.*
Read **Matthew 13:53-58**. Verse 57 tells us, *They took offense at him.*

According to this passage, to what did this offense lead?

_____

What did this prevent Yeshua from doing? _____

Have you dealt with unbelief in your Christian walk? Explain.

_____

_____

In **Mark 9:14-25**, Yeshua met a man struggling with unbelief. What was the man's plea in verse 24?

_____

If this is your struggle, ask Yeshua the same thing. Write your prayer here.

_____

_____

_____

Emerald – Day Five
Life, growth, fresh, and *flourishing*

Heart, Soul, and Mind

As a parent, you may not always approve of your children's behavior, but you still love them no matter what. Your relationship with your children is not based on your changing feelings. I knew my mom and dad loved me even when they disciplined me for disobeying them.

This is the way God sees us. We are His children and His love for us is unconditional and never performance based. When we understand this with our hearts, not just our heads, it allows us to love Him the same way He loves us. He loves you with His heart, soul, and mind. God doesn't ask anything from us that He doesn't already do.

In today's lesson, we continue our study on unbelief but end on a positive note with love.

Scripture often uses the phrase *lack of faith* and the word *unbelief* interchangeably. They use the same Greek root word for *faith* or *pistia*.[14] Unbelief is the word *apistia* meaning *no* or *anti faith*.[15]

In Mark 4:35-40 and Matthew 8:23-26, Yeshua and His disciples crossed the Sea of Galilee. Yeshua calmed the storm that threatened to sink their boat and asked His frightened disciples why they had no faith. This incident caused them to wonder who Yeshua was that even the wind and sea obeyed Him. They believed in Him already, but they lacked the faith He could/would save them.

Mark 6:5-6 and Matthew 13:58 tell us Yeshua could do no miracles in His hometown because of *unbelief*. The people of Nazareth only saw Yeshua as Joseph the carpenter's son, not the Son of God. They did not believe He was deity. Because of this unbelief, Yeshua couldn't perform many healings. Here we see a blatant unbelief that Yeshua was God. This unbelief rendered Yeshua powerless to heal them, because He will never force anything on us, even healing.

We can struggle with doubt, lack of faith, or even unbelief at times, but God knows our weakness. He gives us grace at those times. God understands our struggles and He does not withhold healing because you occasionally doubt. The disciples' lack of faith did not keep Yeshua from calming the storm.

In this next section, please do not feel condemnation. This is an opportunity to examine our lives for areas of unbelief so God can work in us to reveal His power and love. We learn that extreme unbelief leads to rebellion.

It is possible for us, as Christians, to restrict the Son of God and His Holy Spirit by our unbelief. We can go to Yeshua and ask Him to reveal these areas and He will do it without condemnation. He is our source of truth.

We can look for truth in so many places, except in God's Word and His Son. There are many who read all sorts of books looking for truth but never open the Word of God. As impressive as your pastor, Sunday school teacher, or parents and friends are, we are all deceived in one or more areas of our lives and lack faith at times. We must ask our Creator to show us the truth where we doubt and where we embrace unbelief. He must be our go-to person for understanding and truth.

If we jump ahead to **Hebrews 4:6**, we can see that disobedience is the bigger problem. The word for *disobedience* in this verse also means *unbelief*. This is a different Greek word than we saw in the Matthew and Mark events above. This kind of unbelief leads to rebellion.

Unbelief or disobedience unchecked and unrepentant may lead to the hardening of our hearts, which can lead to rebellion. Rebellion is "the action or process of resisting authority, control, or convention."[16] Resisting God's authority is rebellion. God hates rebellion. If this resistance kept the children of Israel from entering God's rest, what will it do to us?

In **Deuteronomy 21:18-21**, if a son was stubborn and rebellious the elders took him out of the city and stoned him.

Why do you think it was punished with such severity?

_____

_____

Please read **Hebrews 3:13**. According to this verse, what hardens us?

_____

When sin is present in our lives, there may be deception. Please do not let sin (or unbelief) harden your heart. He tells us to *exhort [or encourage] one another every day...* Please read **Ezekiel 36:22-27**.

What does God promise He will do for the sake of His holy name?

_____

_____

Look back at **Hebrews 3:14**. Here is how the New Living Translation (NLT) translates it: *For if we are faithful to the end, trusting God just as firmly as when we first believed, we will share in all that belongs to Christ* (emphasis mine). Why did the author say this? Because they were in danger of *falling away* (Heb. 3:12). He wants His readers to trust God as much as the day they first loved Him. There is another church in Scripture to whom Yeshua gave a similar command.

Please read **Revelation 2:1-5**. Yeshua had a message for the church in Ephesus. What was it?

_____

_____

What is the greatest Commandment? In **Matthew 22:37** we read, *You shall love the Lord your God with all your heart and with all your soul and with all your mind.* This is the New Testament version of the words Moses wrote in **Deuteronomy 6:5**.

Heart, soul, and mind.

I want to define each of these for you. The Greek word meaning heart denotes a reference to the areas of the inner self, including the volition, the mind, the desires, etc.[17] The Greek word for soul means, "the seat of the feelings, desires, affections, aversions."[18] Last, the Greek word for mind means *understanding, feeling, desiring.*[19]

Moses loved God this way. More importantly, this is the way Yeshua loves His Father, and *He* is our example. Loving God in this way requires sacrifice. Sacrifice and surrender of our time, love, energy, and life. Our entire being!

Is there anything keeping you from loving God with all your heart, soul, and mind? What is it?

_____

_____

Remember, God doesn't ask anything from us that He doesn't do. Ask Him to help you love Him more.

What verses led you to the beautiful green of the emerald?

_____

Yeshua is our emerald of life. He gives us His water and became our Bread of Life so we can grow and flourish in Him. Next time you see an emerald, remember how Yeshua has given you life.

Write any thoughts, prayers, or comments about this chapter. What has God shown you, or how has He healed you through His Word?

_____

_____

_____

_____

Chapter 4 - Onyx
Judgment, the fear of the Lord, and mourning

Day One

It's believed a South African man has an onyx stone that has been missing for 1,000 years. The writing on it is in an ancient script that dates to 1000 B.C., and it is thought to be one of the stones found on each shoulder of the breastplate worn by the high priest.[1] The script appears to be one letter or word, but according to the Bible, the stones on the priest's shoulders had the names of the twelve tribes inscribed on them. The Urim and Thummim were stones the high priest kept behind the ephod to inquire of God (I will explain more on this later). These stones may have had one word on them, according to the Talmud, or the Oral Torah, because they were used to ask "yes" or "no" questions of God.

Alexander the Great and other rulers used onyx for cameos.[2] Genesis 2:12 describes the four rivers coming out of Eden, and the land surrounded by the first river has gold, bdellium (a pearl-like resin), and onyx. Since this stone has a deep black hue with white, its color symbolizes *judgment, the fear of the Lord, and mourning.*[3]

I have had many Greek influences throughout my life. In high school, I had a Greek teacher for anatomy who was tough. His personality could be harsh, but it was to push you further than you thought you could go.

Years later, I worked in cancer research, and a doctor from Greece joined our lab. Although he was friendly and outgoing, he knew how he wanted things and would not take "no" for an answer. Sometimes that caused problems.

Later, I dated a guy who attended my church. He was a dark, cute, outgoing medical student. He and his family were Greek, and his mother had come to the States when she was nineteen years old. There is a word in Greek applied to non-family members and non-Greeks; it is xénos, meaning stranger or foreigner. My boyfriend was a mamma's boy, and his mamma didn't like me; I was xénos. That caused problems.

After we broke up, my friend set me up on a blind date. This guy was coming from Cleveland to my roommate's bridal shower, and they thought it a good idea to introduce me to him over dinner. We talked about our jobs, dogs, and our mutual love for peanut butter and jelly. Then the announcement: my friend spoke up and said, "Hey Stephanie, did you know Mike is Greek?" Silence. *He has red hair… he can't be,* I thought. I had sworn off Greeks. No way was I going out with another Greek mamma's boy.

Ah, but he won me over. His mamma did, too.

I have learned much of the Greek culture, language, and people from my husband and his family, which has helped me in my study of the New Testament. This may be one reason the Lord put so many Greek people in my life. In the last few years, the Lord has made the switch to Jewish people… I think you will see why as we go through this study.

At the end of Chapter 3, we looked at **Matthew 22:37**. As I mentioned before, this verse comes from **Deuteronomy 6:5**. When you read the Old Testament verse, it says, *You shall love the LORD your God with all your heart and with all your soul and with all your might.* As stated earlier, Matthew uses the word *mind,* instead of *might.* In **Mark 12:29-30**, Jesus says, *Hear, O Israel, the Lord our God, the Lord is one. And you shall love the Lord your God with all your heart and with all your soul and with all your mind and with all your strength.* Mark includes heart, soul, mind, and strength. Why do I compare these similar verses?

Because of the difference in Hebrew vs. Greek (or Hebraic vs. Hellenistic) thinking and learning.

The Hebrew word for *might* means, "Exceedingly, much, force, abundance."[4] The Hebrew word for heart includes the heart and mind because the Hebraic way is to think with your heart. Greeks used heart and mind separately because intellect and thought were most important.

Why should we care about this? Because we read a Bible written by Jews who spoke and wrote Hebrew as their first language, followed the Torah, and lived in Israel. We worship a Savior born a Jew, who taught in the Temple, observed every Sabbath and Feast, spoke Hebrew, and not only knew and followed the Torah, but GAVE the Torah to His people, too. Do you think it matters to Him we understand His cultural and spiritual ways as well?

In Hebrew, more of their words are verbs compared to Greek, which are nouns. Why? *Because the Hebraic way is about doing, not just knowing.* Much of our religious culture is about understanding doctrine, theology, and denominational beliefs. This was not the Church in the first few hundred years after Yeshua ascended to Heaven. *It was about doing what Yeshua taught.* That is why He spent so much time with people, to be an example of what *to do*, not what *to think*.

Maybe having the *mind of Christ* includes more than trying to think like the Son of God. Perhaps it involves doing, acting, and learning as He did as a Jewish boy. Remember, Judaism and Christianity were the same thing at the time of Yeshua and were never meant to be separate "religions." It was Yeshua's people (the tribe of Judah) who rejected Him and refused to let the Jews and Gentiles become one in Christ. Yeshua came to fulfill Judaism (and the Law) and make it complete.

Most of us think and learn in the style of the Greeks. If you saw the movie *My Big, Fat, Greek Wedding*, it resembles my life. For twenty-five years, my husband has been explaining one thing or another by saying, "It comes from the Greek word…"

Our culture, including our schools and churches, has been and still is heavily influenced by the Greeks. As a result, to understand Yeshua and His Word we must appreciate His Hebrew roots, and ours.

In his book, *God in Search of Man*, Abraham Heschel writes, "The Greeks learned to comprehend. The Hebrews learned to revere. The modern man learns to use."[5] I think revering and loving Him is what God wants from us most. Do you read and study Scripture to experience, hear, and love Him more? We miss so much by trying to make the Bible fit our purposes and worldview instead of just doing what Yeshua did: *living for God and loving Him first above everything and everyone.* Yeshua is our example of doing what Deuteronomy, Matthew, and Mark say, *Love the Lord your God with all your heart, soul, mind, and strength.* He modeled it by *doing* everything the Father told Him to do.

Loving is a verb, so is believing. Believe is what we must do to be saved, right? It is not about what we think, rather more about what *we do*. Let me say it again. Believing in the biblical, Hebraic way is what we do, *not* what we ponder. We may feel believing starts in the head, but it begins in the heart. Everything we learn about Yeshua and God's Word begins in our intellect and understanding, but it should not stay there. It needs to become heart knowledge.

How can you turn what you *understand* (intellectually) about Yeshua into what your heart *knows* (believes) about Yeshua?

_____

_____

Onyx – Day Two
Judgment, the fear of the Lord, and mourning

Obedience is Best

Years ago, I was starting a women's Bible study at my church. As I prayed, God gave me direction for the study I was to teach, when I was to teach it, and who to invite. As I began putting all the pieces together and inviting people in my community, a friend suggested a different study by a well-known Bible teacher. She raved about how good it was and how it would benefit the women in our church. Being a people-pleaser, I told her I would investigate it.

That evening, I pulled out the book she loaned me and began to read the introduction. The Holy Spirit stopped me in my tracks. He spoke to my heart and said, "That is not the study I want you to teach. Are you going to be obedient to Me?" I was taken aback. I had never heard His voice like that. But I said, "Yes, I will do what You want me to do," and closed the book. I gave it back to my friend and explained to her how God really wanted me to do the other study.

In today's lesson, you will read about the consequences of disobedience. You will also see Yeshua in the Old Testament, where you might not have expected to see Him.

Before moving on to Hebrews 4, let's look at **Hebrews 3:18-19**.

According to these verses, who could not enter God's rest?

_____

The author uses the words *disobedient* and *unbelief* to describe the same group of people God refused to let enter His rest (the Promised Land). Being obedient is the "doing" of belief. Does that make sense? We are obedient because we believe who God is, in His promises, and what He says.

There is another example of this in **Matthew 19:16-22**. Read these verses and note the first question the rich, young man asks. Write it here:

_____
_____

At first, Yeshua doesn't respond to the "doing" part of the question, only the "good" part. Yeshua tells him to *keep* the commandments. The word *keep* means "to observe, to guard, to attend to, or take care of."[6]
Now, read verse 21, what does Yeshua say to him?

_____
_____

Many versions of the Bible have the phrase "If you would be perfect..." The word *perfect* used here means "finished, complete, or mature."[7] **Hebrews 2:10** uses the same word when it says, *For it was fitting that he [God]... should make the founder of our salvation perfect through suffering.* God made Yeshua perfect or complete, in His human form, through suffering. Yeshua wanted to make the rich, young man perfect, too.

To obtain maturity or completeness in our faith, we must do as Yeshua asks (obedience). Everyone is different, and Yeshua knew what this man was holding onto that kept him from maturing or reaching perfection in his faith. I believe He asks us to *do something* or *give* Him the thing that keeps us from maturity or completeness.

To what possession, dream, relationship, or desire are you holding? Be honest. Give it to Yeshua. Your obedience shows your belief and trust in Him.

_____

_____

Hebrews 4 continues with the theme of unbelief from Hebrews 3 by using the word, *therefore*. (You may need to review Hebrews 3, so this chapter makes more sense.)

Please read **Hebrews 4:1-7**.

In verse 1, the promise of rest still stands. According to **Psalm 95** (Heb. 3:7-11), rest refers to the land of Canaan.

What rest do you think the author is referring to in **Hebrews 4:1**? Why?

_____

_____

I believe this is referring to God's rest. His salvation. The *Messianic Jewish Bible* states **Hebrews 4:1** this way: *Let us fear then! Though a promise of entering his rest is still open, some of you would seem to have fallen short.*

What could have caused their failure to reach this rest? (You may need to go back to Hebrews 3).

_____

_____

Now, I want to take you back to the story of Moses and the Promised Land in **Exodus 23:20-33**. I know this may be a lot to read, but it will help you understand this chapter of Hebrews.

Look at **Exodus 23:20-22**. Have you ever read something similar? Whom does this angel sound like? What does God warn them against?

_____

_____

_____

_____

God is sending the Children of Israel to a place He has prepared for them, by an "angel" who has his name in Him. The Good News is the rest God gave referred to in **Hebrews 4:2**.

Now go with me to **Numbers 14:1-12**. This chapter picks up after the spies Moses sent into Canaan (their Promised Land) returned with their report of giants in the land.

How did the Children of Israel respond?

_____

_____

Please read a bit more. Stay in **Numbers 14** and continue reading verses **26-38**. This will help you understand what we have been studying in Hebrews.

How does God respond to the Children of Israel?

_____

_____

This rebellion is what Psalm 95:7-11 is referring to in Hebrews 3. *Disobedience* is precisely what the author is warning his readers against.

Hebrews 4:2 says, *[The children of Israel] were not united by faith with those who listened [to God and looked forward to the Promised Land].* God told them to obey the voice of the Angel He sent ahead of them, and their enemies would be His. He would drive them out of the land. Wow! This promise is still real today. Do you realize that?

God loves us so much. He does not want us to fail or be overtaken by *the enemy*. When we are submissive to His leading, our enemies become His. Not one person or thing can stop us from taking the land He has promised us.

Onyx – Day Three
Judgment, the fear of the Lord, and *mourning*

Shabbat Shalom (Sabbath Peace)

I love Sundays and look forward to them all week. I do not feel the least bit guilty for sitting on the couch with a good book or watching a good movie after Sunday worship and lunch. The Sabbath may mean something different to you.

I grew up not being allowed to do laundry on Sunday or any other work, except dishes, I always had to do the dishes… It was the day of rest, and we took it in all its legalistic glory. Now, I have different views of the Sabbath but still see it as a day of rest. Worship is part of our rest, as you will see.

Let's get started by reading **Hebrews 4:1-3**.

Rest. What does it mean to you?

_____

_____

_____

Some scholars believe this scripture is from an eternal perspective meaning Heaven, others think it's concerning salvation through Christ; still others believe it refers to the Millennial Kingdom. Maybe to you, the word rest means never having to fight another battle (from an eternal perspective) or taking the day off (from a weekly standpoint).

Let's resume reading Hebrews 4.

Hebrews 4:3-11 continues the topic of rest. Most of us think of the Sabbath as the day we attend church. You may go on Saturday or Sunday and believe as long as you attend church, you are keeping the Sabbath. I thought this for many years. I want to take you to Exodus to read how God described the Sabbath to Moses.

Please read **Exodus 20:8-11**. This passage comes from the Ten Commandments.

I have a good friend who is a pastor and teacher, and she gave a sermon concerning the Sabbath. She made a point of asking, if we believe we are to keep the Ten Commandments, why don't we keep the Sabbath? Is it because we do not feel that the Sabbath applies to us? It's a Jewish thing, right? If the other nine refer to us, why doesn't keeping the Sabbath pertain to us, too?

Next, read **Exodus 31:12-18.** In these verses, God gives us more detail about the Sabbath. In the very first verse, we learn why we are to keep the Sabbath. Also, think of the Sabbath from the Hebraic perspective as the doing, not the thinking way of things.

According to this verse, why did God command His people to keep the Sabbath?

_____

_____

God doesn't want us to reflect or consider the things He commands. He wants us to do them. The Hebrew word for *hear* means to obey. [8]

In **Exodus 31:13**, God wants us to keep (or to remember) the Sabbath so we may know He sanctifies us. He says in verse 14, *You shall keep the Sabbath because it is holy for you*. Why is this important?

God wants us to be His light. He wants us to be different. How can we be a light to the world if we are as tired and overworked as the rest of our culture? If each day is like another, how do we show the world we are set apart? How do we display our Sabbath is as holy to us as God said?

When I visited Israel, the group I went with was fortunate enough to be part of a Shabbat (Hebrew

Sabbath) meal. Shabbat is twenty-five hours long and includes turning off electronics (yes, all of them), spending time at the synagogue (at the time of Yeshua, they recited Psalm 95:7-11 every week on Shabbat), and spending time in the Torah with God and family. Friends and family members eat a meal consisting of many courses. Dinner begins with a blessing and breaking bread representing peace from any conflict occurring during the week. Next, the man of the house recites a blessing over a glass of wine or grape juice, demonstrating the sanctification of the day of rest. It is like Communion.

At one point during the meal, the man of the house sings Proverbs 31 to his wife to bless and honor her. He and his wife then take the faces of each of their children in their hands and speak blessings over them individually. The looks on their children's faces were priceless!

Let me summarize this for you. Every week, an Orthodox Jewish family gives reverence and praise to God, makes peace with God and family, blesses and honors the women and children, all while resting from work and spending time together reading the Word. How different our families would be if we kept the Sabbath like this, instead of just hurrying to church.

This is an example of being set apart, not like the world but living out devotion, faith, honor, obedience, and rest.

The Hellenistic (Greek) way of keeping the Sabbath would be about my rest, my day off, and what I want to do to enjoy it. This is not at all what God meant by the Sabbath. The Hebraic way is about God, family, and friends—in that order.

Furthermore, in **Exodus 31:13-18**, God has not put us to death for not keeping the Sabbath in the way He spoke of in these verses, and I don't want to be legalistic about it either. However, God wants us to rest because we need a DAY of rest. Does that mean you can't throw a load of laundry in the washer and dryer? No. That is legalism. What the Lord says here is *to rest*. Plain and simple, we need rest. Our bodies were created to heal, rebuild, and reproduce (at a cellular level) during rest.

I teach biology and anatomy to home-schooled students. When we get to mitosis and meiosis, or cell division/reproduction, there is a phase called interphase. During this stage of mitosis, the cell rests. Throughout this rest, the cell is preparing to do considerable replication and division, and without this rest, cell division could not happen. Every cell in your body, which is in the trillions, divides and gives rise to two new cells so it can replace every organ, bone, and muscle every seven years or so. New skin cells are made as others die off, and your red blood cells get replaced every 120 days. Your heart never stops beating but must rest between each beat. If it fails to relax between beats, it seizes, and you have a heart attack. Muscles and nerves cannot continually contract or fire but must have a recovery period. The human body has latent intervals (rest) built in at a cellular level.

Your heart, soul, mind, and body need to rest. Why? *So, you can give them to God and love Him with all of you.*

Onyx – Day Four
Judgment, the fear of the Lord, and *mourning*

Today, we will finish our lesson on the Sabbath and begin a new lesson on "The Living and Active Word." Please read **Hebrews 4:1-11**.

At the end of verse 7 in Hebrews 4, the author writes, *Today, if you hear his voice, do not harden your hearts*. Let's start by asking the Lord for a soft heart so we will be sensitive to the Holy Spirit's leading.

Turn to **Exodus 31:17**. God said, *It is a sign forever between me and the people of Israel that in six days the LORD made heaven and earth, and on the seventh day he rested and was refreshed*. We see in this passage God Himself rested and was refreshed. Remember, you may not be from Israel or even Jewish, but as a believer, God grafted you into the family tree and you became a child of Abraham and God. This verse applies to all of us.

In **Hebrews 4:8-11,** Joshua's rest is referred to. Turn to **Joshua 5:10-12**. What "rest" did Joshua give?

_____

_____

Joshua did not give the same rest as God provides. The rest Joshua gave was the Promised Land, because they could finally rest from wandering through the wilderness. But it was a shadow and practice of what was to come through Yeshua. Wandering the desert symbolizes our sin. Our rest comes from His salvation.

We see shadows, types, and practices many, many times throughout the Torah and the rest of the Old Testament writings. God had them practice the things Yeshua would bring. Yeshua is the Lord of the Sabbath; works compare to the Law.

Please read **Hebrews 4:10-11** again. For what are we to strive?

_____

_____

In the spiritual sense of the word, God gives us rest through His Son. As God rested from His works, we can rest from the works (sacrifices, practices, and offerings) of the Law because we have grace.

Turn to **Ephesians 2:8-9**. Replace the word *works* (in verse 9) with the phrase *the Law*. As a result of works or the Law, what happens? _____

However, we are saved through faith. In Greek, this means "a conviction or belief (a noun)."[9]

Conversely, in Hebrew, faith means "to nourish, to make firm and strong (a verb)."[10] See the difference? One is a noun while the other is a verb (doing).

Yeshua saves (*sozo* - to make well, heal, restore to health) by grace (favor, mercy, kindness) through faith (nourishing to make firm and strong)[11], while the Law (or works) produces boasting.

In **Hebrews 4:11**, why does the author say, *So no one may fall by the same disobedience*? (The answer to this goes back to verses 4-7).

_____

_____

Now, let's read a familiar verse. Chances are you have heard or read **Hebrews 4:12** many times.

Let me say two things about this verse. First, please read it in the context of Hebrews 4. It can be a stand-alone verse, but you will find more meaning when you read it in the perspective of the other verses around it. Second, remember there was no Bible at the time of this writing. The only Word they had was Yeshua and the Tanakh, or Scriptures.

In Hebrew, *word* means the "spoken word or speech."[12] So, the *word of God* in this text is the very words out of God's mouth. Everything He has ever said, either written or spoken to your heart.

On a side note, in **Luke 21:33,** when Yeshua said, *Heaven and earth will pass away, but my words shall never pass away,* I believe this has a similar meaning. This verse is not talking about the Bible as we know it, but every word the Father and Son have spoken.

Please read **Hebrews 4:12**. How is the word of God described?

_____

_____

Let's look at a few of these words. First, the word *living* is just what it sounds like: God's words are alive, and they give life. As I was thinking about this word, the Lord dropped so many Scriptures into my heart. Verses describing Yeshua such as *I am the Bread of Life* (**John 6:35**), *Living water* (**John 4:10**), *Eternal Life, Author of Life,* (**Acts 3:15**), *The Living one* (**Rev. 1:18**)...

I'm sure you can think of some, too. Record any verses or names include the word living, life, or alive.

_____

_____

_____

Onyx – Day Five
Judgment, the fear of the Lord, and mourning

The Living and Active Word

These days devotionals and self-help books are all the rage. Many Christians use them for their quiet time each morning. However, we must be careful not to let them *replace* God's Word. I'm not talking about a book that quotes Scripture, but the BOOK itself. We need to be in God's Word; reading what God says to us through His Holy Spirit. It is possible to inherit the theology of many authors, causing the truth to get lost.

In day four, we saw how God's Word is living. Today, we continue our lesson about the living and active word.

The next word in **Hebrews 4:12** is *active,* and it comes from the Greek word *enarges,* which looks like the English word *energy* and means "evident, clear, and visible."[13] The King James Version translates it as *powerful.*

Please look up **Isaiah 55:10-11**. To what is God's word being compared? What will it *do*?

_____

_____

_____

God's words are to achieve something in our heart and life; they are not just to be contemplated. They are life-giving. I told you earlier the Greeks thought with their minds and the Hebrews thought with their hearts. We need to let God's Word become more than head knowledge; it needs to be heart knowledge.

God's Word is sharper than a sword, able to *pierce* through the soul and spirit. The word *pierce* means "to penetrate or get through."[14] This may be one reason we may not like to read the Bible. Just the sound of the word *pierce* sounds painful, right? It conjures up thoughts of knives, needles, wounds, and other unpleasant things. However, it may remind you of a new piercing you want in your ear or cartilage. (Although I hear those things can be painful as well.) But I digress. Unless the Word penetrates our heart, we will not grow and change.

Our soul is our mind, will, and emotions, and our spirit is the very thing our Creator breathed into us. Both are eternal and God-given, and often they are at war with one another. Our spirit communes with God through the Holy Spirit while our soul is everything that makes us who we are.

So, why would the Word divide them? God wants us to be Spirit-driven, not soul-driven. The Spirit is love, peace, truth. It is patient, gentle, kind, self-controlled, faithful, and joyful. This is where God wants us to live and function. The soul can be moody, self-centered, turbulent, depressed, thoughtless, self-driven, lacking self-control, and deceitful. Satan can influence our souls by manipulating our thoughts. If we are not in the Word of Truth, under the perfect power of the Spirit of Truth, we get off track.

God wants us to be Spirit-led and Word-led. One without the other is only half of the equation. Unfortunately, many overdo one or the other. We become so Spirit-led we assume everything we think is of the Holy Spirit and will act and speak out without the guidelines of the Word. However, being overly Word-lead can stifle or quench the Holy Spirit so we can no longer hear Him, because everything becomes an intellectual experience. The Holy Spirit is soft-spoken. Do you realize that? He will not over-talk you; we must be quiet and listen. I think this is where the phrase "quiet time" originated. There needs to be a balance. Seek Yeshua, ask Him, and He will teach you how.

What are practical ways we can avoid being unbalanced in the Spirit or the Word?

_____
_____

Next, this verse says God's Word is a discerner or a judge of thoughts and intentions. In Greek, this word is not a verb but an adjective. Why does it matter, you ask? *Because it means the words of God are skilled at judging or discerning.* We could put it this way: The discerning (judging) Word of God is living and active. Judging is what it is, not what it does. God's words are meant to reveal our hearts. When God speaks to my heart, there is no doubt in my mind what He means. He can discern the motives, intentions, and thoughts behind what I say and do. God will correct me, too. He makes Himself clear without condemnation; He speaks in love.

Please read **Hebrews 4:13**. Don't let this verse intimidate you. Also, read **Psalm 33:13-15**. This is another way to understand the verse in Hebrews 4:13.

How do you think **Hebrews 4:13** relates to verses 11 and 12 above it?

_____
_____
_____

Remember, the author of Hebrews is dealing with the unbelief, turning away, and disobedience of the people to whom he is writing. He reminds us God sees our hearts, and all things under the sun. Not one thing can escape His sight. These words can be comforting when we are trying to live a righteous life with Yeshua as our Savior and example, but they can be a little unnerving if we are trying to do it without Him.

There is no way around the fact we are all accountable for every action and thought. However, the author of Hebrews does not leave us at that point; he tells us the good news in the very next section. You should already know it is Yeshua! He is our righteousness; He stands in our place, interceding for us.

Where was the onyx? What verse or verses uncovered it? The onyx is a dark, beautiful stone. When the Word exposes our hearts, we can be free from everything that holds us back from letting Yeshua rule in our lives.

_____
_____

Is there anything the Holy Spirit revealed to you in this chapter regarding rest or God's Word?

_____
_____

Does it help to understand the difference between the Greek and Hebrew ways of learning and thinking? How can you incorporate more of the Hebraic learning style into your study of the Bible?

_____
_____

Chapter 5 – Sapphire
Heaven, the priesthood, revelation, and the Jehovah color

Day One

The sapphire is my favorite gem and color! My husband will tell you I would have blue everywhere if I could. Since it is my birthstone, Mike gave me a lovely ring during our first year of marriage. I wear it often because it is my favorite gift from him.

The most famous sapphire of recent history is the engagement ring of Lady Diana given to her by Prince Charles of England. It was a twelve-carat sapphire surrounded by fourteen diamonds and white gold.[1] She was as famous and beautiful as her ring. After her untimely death, her son, Prince William, received it and his wife, Kate, now wears it.

It is a valuable and hard gem with a hardness rating of nine. Scripture uses it to describe Heaven or the Throne of God. (Ex. 24:10, Ez. 1:26, 10:1). A website on sapphires says it signifies the divine nature of God and His character.[2] The blue hue symbolizes *Heaven, the priesthood,* and *revelation* (not the book), and it's the "Jehovah color."[3]

In Chapter 4, we ended with verse 13 which said, *And no creature is hidden from his sight, but all are naked and exposed to the eyes of him to whom we must give account.* Even though this verse may leave us feeling intimidated or convicted, the good news comes in **Hebrews 4:14-16**. Please read these verses.

Because of our inability to hide from God and having to give an account for all we have done, the phrase "Since then," used to begin **Hebrews 4:14**, introduces the importance of our Great High Priest.

We will explore the job and functions of the high priests and priesthood in more detail. However, for now, understand the high priest was a mediator between God and man. God sees Yeshua as our Great High Priest, standing in our place, concealing our imperfections with His righteousness. This is a beautiful assurance for you and me!

In **Hebrews 4:15**, what is one of the most important characteristics of our High Priest?

_____

_____

As stated in Chapter 2, according to the Torah, the high priest would go into the Holy of Holies once a year on the Day of Atonement or Yom Kippur. Before sacrificing a goat for the people of Israel, he would sacrifice a bull for his sin (Lev. 16). They atoned for their sin first. Yeshua never had to do that! He is sinless and perfect, yet He sympathizes with (or understands) our weaknesses because He was tempted in every way we are.

In what area of your life do you want to be an overcomer? Yeshua knows because He was tempted with that, too. Record it here or in a journal. There is no condemnation in Yeshua. He will free you.

Commit it to prayer and even fasting if the Lord leads you in that direction.

_____

_____

Why do you think **Hebrews 4:16** opens with the words, *Let us then*?

_____

_____

We can approach the throne of God, our Creator and Lord, with boldness or confidence. The Greek word used for *boldness* or confidence means "freedom in speaking, unreservedness in speech, openly, frankly."[4] Because Yeshua understands us, we can speak honestly concerning our struggles, sins, problems, strongholds, temptations, relationships, etc. Do you think, by not confessing something to God, you are keeping it a secret? God *wants* to help you. He *desires* to free you.

What happens when we approach God's throne this way?

_____

You have heard it said, "Grace is when God gives us what we don't deserve, and mercy is when God doesn't give us what we deserve." Notice in **Hebrews 4:16**, we **receive** mercy, and **find** grace. The difference between these two words is receiving means to take with the hand, so someone gives it to you, *finding* means to come upon something with or without searching. As we approach the Throne of God in prayer, confessing our sin and seeking Him, we may think God will condemn and heap guilt on us, but, instead, He will hand us mercy and we will find the one thing we don't deserve, grace. *All this because Yeshua is our mediator and High Priest. Therefore, there is now no condemnation for those who are in Christ.* (Rom. 8:1).

Hebrews 5 continues with the theme of the high priest. Read **Hebrews 5:1-4**.
Verse 1 gives the primary function of a high priest: *He is appointed to act on behalf of men…*
From the beginning, people were unaware of their need for a mediator or advocate. Believing ourselves to be self-reliant and independent makes it easier to deny a Creator than to admit we need someone to mediate between God and us. Fortunately, God knows our poverty better than we do.

God appointed the high priests when He chose Aaron, Moses' brother to be the first high priest and the men of his lineage to continue to be priests forever.

When He gave the Torah to Moses, God set up a system of priests to perform sacrifices for sin on behalf of the Israelites. Without this, the Lord would have destroyed them for their disobedience and other sins. This human high priest was different because God appointed and set him apart to perform these functions. He was as weak and sinful as the next man. This, however, was also in God's plan.

In **Hebrews 5:2,** why is it important the high priest have his own weaknesses?

_____

_____

Let's examine the functions and purposes of the priesthood in the Old Testament and see more reasons Yeshua is our Great High Priest.

Exodus 28 describes the high priest and priests' garments. I realize it may be a lot to read, but this passage is very descriptive and fascinating. It strikes me how God wanted these garments to be for glory and beauty. Even though **Isaiah 53:2** tells us, *[Yeshua] had no form or majesty that we should look at him, and no beauty that we should desire him*, this Scripture refers to the time of His life on Earth. When we read His description in **Revelation 1:12-16**, we see a vastly different depiction.

How does John, the author of Revelation, react in verse 17?

_____

John's reaction was not to a man without majesty or splendor. In His heavenly, royal form, Yeshua is full of glory and magnificence.

In **Exodus 28:2**, what did God want Aaron's garments to do for him?

_____

_____

The words consecrate or sanctify can mean *ordained*, too. We see this word used in John 10:35-36. Keep your place in **Exodus 28** but read **John 10:35-36**.

What did the Father do before sending Yeshua out into the world?

_____

Who and what God uses, He sanctifies, whether it is His Son, His priests, their garments, you, or me. God set us apart on purpose so He can make us holy. Many times during my life, I have felt as though I didn't fit in. It wasn't as though I couldn't get along with people either. I didn't want to do what they did or go where they went. Going to church, being in Bible studies, and reading books that helped me grow closer to Yeshua was enjoyable. A friend liked to call me a "Jesus freak;" I am still unsure if she meant it as a compliment.

We cannot live with one foot in the world and one foot in the Kingdom of God. We will be ineffective in both worlds. Either God has set you apart, or He hasn't. In our flesh, we don't want to be different, but God calls us to be separate.

Throughout Scripture and today, God desires His own be a light to the world. We are to show them how *being godly* looks. However, it is easy to talk like the world, act like the world, and see and listen to everything the world promotes. Please do not mistake what I am saying for legalism or condemnation. God wants us to have a pure heart for Him. I am talking about loving what He loves and hating what He hates. If you honestly don't know what God loves and hates, read your Bible and ask the Holy Spirit to give you wisdom in this area.

What area do you need wisdom? Maybe you need to ask God to show you areas in your life where you are loving something He hates. Will you ask Him now?

_____

_____

_____

Sapphire – Day Two
Heaven, the priesthood, revelation, and *the Jehovah color*

My dad died a month after I got married in 1992. Right after his death, a friend gave me a small plaque with a tribute to a father. It begins with, *Thank you, Dad for what you've done to build our family...* It's the type of present you may give your dad on Father's Day. Every time I read it, I think of my dad. It's my memorial to his life now that he is no longer here. In today's lesson, we will read about a remembrance God set up for Himself.

Return to **Exodus 28.** We find in verses 6-14 how Moses was to have the ephod for the priests made. This was a thing of beauty, but, more importantly, it was a symbol of commemoration.

What was on the ephod?

_____

Before discussing this in more detail, let's read about the next garment found in **Exodus 28:15-30.** The breastplate of judgment was made to look like the ephod but was smaller and fit across the chest over the heart.

What are set in the breastplate, and what is their significance?

_____

All twelve tribes of Israel were before God every time Aaron went into the Holy Place. They were represented on the garments he wore before God in the Tabernacle. This was still significant during the period of Yeshua's ministry. Think about these things: How many disciples did Yeshua have (Mark 3:14-19)? After feeding the 5,000, how many baskets of bread and fish did Yeshua have left (John 6:1-13)?

In **Revelation 21:12-21**, we see the city of New Jerusalem coming from Heaven. It has a wall with twelve gates, twelve pearls (one for each gate), and twelve angels (one on each gate), and each of the names of the twelve tribes will be on the gates. It has twelve foundations with the names of the twelve disciples on them. The wall measurements are in multiples of twelve, and twelve different stones adorn its foundations. Can we assume this number is significant to God? How can anyone believe Christians have replaced the Jews as God's chosen people? He loves them, and they are a remembrance before Him always.

The high priests often served as judges for the people. Immediately after His arrest, guards took Yeshua to Annas, the former high priest. Next, they brought him to Annas' son-in-law Caiaphas, the current high priest, where he questioned Yeshua and found Him guilty of blasphemy (John 18, Matt. 26).

Please turn to and read **Matthew 25:31-46** and **2 Corinthians 5:10-11**, what do these verses reveal to us about Yeshua?

_____

_____

We read in **Exodus 28:30** Aaron had two stones inside the breastplate of judgment. He used these stones to rule for the people of Israel in the Holy Place. One stone, called the Urim, meant *lights,* and the other, Thummim, represented *perfection.* Because he bore the judgment of the people on his heart, we consider Aaron a type and shadow of the Messiah.

John 1:6-9 says:

There was a man sent from God, whose name was John. He came as a witness, to bear witness about the light, that all might believe through him. He was not the light but came to bear witness about the light. The true light, which gives light to everyone, was coming into the world.

Yeshua is the light. He is our judge because He is the light who exposes our works (John 3:19-21 ESV).

As we read in **Hebrews 2:10**, suffering perfected Yeshua. **1 Corinthians 13:8-10** says when the *perfect* or *perfection* comes, we will know fully what we only know in part now. That perfect or perfection may apply to the time of Yeshua's returning, or to the New Heaven and Earth, but it refers to Yeshua. He is perfection, and so is everything He does and makes. His judgment is perfect because He is perfect. The Urim and Thummim stones are, therefore, a shadow of Yeshua's judgment. Our Great High Priest who bore our judgment is our Light and the Perfecter of our faith.

We have discussed Exodus 28:33-35, so let's move on to **Exodus 28:36-38**. Please read **Exodus 39:30** and **Leviticus 8:9**, too.

By what other name is the plate of pure gold called?

_____

What is engraved on this plate?

_____

Look at verse 38 in Exodus 28. Here is the same verse in the New Living Translation:

Aaron will wear it [the plate of gold] on his forehead, thus bearing the guilt connected with any errors regarding the sacred offerings of the people of Israel. He must always wear it so the Lord will accept the people.

Aaron and his garments were dedicated for service to the Lord. He was *Holy to the Lord (Ex. 28:36)*, not only to do the Lord's work but so God accepted the people of Israel. Aaron would bear the guilt of the people for any mistakes they made as they presented their required gifts to the Lord. This is why he was "Holy to the Lord." Only that which is holy in God's sight can bear the guilt of another.

Do you see how Yeshua lived this? Do you understand why Aaron is a type and shadow of Yeshua? Yeshua took our guilt so God can accept us.

Please read **Revelation 19:11-12.** We see Yeshua returning to Earth for His Second Coming. Notice what is on His head. We do not know what was written because it is only known to Yeshua. I imagine it is a name the Father gave Him for His obedience to the cross.

What our Conduct says about Us.

Now, we will take a bit of a detour that will continue into tomorrow's study. It is still on topic, but we will examine this same concept differently. Be patient because these verses are rich in meaning, and I want you to grasp it. There is more reading, so please stay with me. First, let's go to **1 Peter 1:13-25**. This section deals with the calling to be holy. Don't worry; we will take this part in small bites.

In **1 Peter 1:15**, how are we to be holy? _____

Think about this verse and your answer. What is your conduct like? How do you act in public? How do you behave at home? Do you feel entitled when visiting retail businesses or restaurants?

Sapphire - Day Three
Heaven, the priesthood, revelation, and *the Jehovah color*

My husband's parents owned a restaurant for over fifty years. My husband worked there his whole life and owned/managed it for thirty-three years. After we married, he asked me to help him run the business after we added computers and extra staff.

Customer behavior shocked me. I loved our regulars. I would go table to table chatting with those I saw weekly or more often. It was enjoyable to make new friends, too. However, there were times it was unbearable. Not only was the work hectic, but occasionally, we got a customer we could not please.

One incident that comes to mind was a group of nicely dressed businessmen. They seemed polite as they ordered their food, but when they had to wait longer for their food on a busy weekend night, one man threw his beverage all over the server.

We constantly had to replace our dinnerware, glasses, menus, and even toilet paper because of theft. I won't mention the things people will do for a free meal. Unfortunately, we saw the worst in people over food. After being screamed at for the first time, I wanted to quit. But that was not the last time someone shouted at me.

If that wasn't bad enough, food from our freezers walked out the back door with an employee every so often. We had one cashier who rarely rang up a takeout sale of candy, coffee, soup, or sodas, because she pocketed the money. As you may imagine, money from our cash drawer disappeared, too. It was hard to understand why these things happened when some of these same people spoke of being Christians.

We knew a couple from a church we attended who liked to go out to eat with us. Most times, the husband was after a free meal. As believers and followers of Yeshua, we need to outshine the world. Sadly, our public behavior can show our sense of entitlement.

Let's continue this lesson on our conduct in 1 Peter.

1 Peter 1:17 states, *If you call on him as Father who judges impartially according to each one's deeds...* Meaning, the one who judges everyone justly by his or her actions, *is the same one you call Father.*

If we call him Father, how are we to conduct ourselves?

_____

1 Peter 1:18-19 tells us why we should conduct ourselves with fear. Explain.

_____

_____

Fear, used in verse 17, means to fear discipline from the Father. This fear is to deter us from bad behavior. The same kind I had as a child when my parents wanted me to understand the consequences of poor conduct. We are all children of our Father, and He disciplines those He loves (Pr. 3:11-12). He does not discipline in a cruel, abusive way but out of love to keep us from being judged for those deeds. Do you understand? *He corrects us to prevent from having to judge us later.*

He wants us to be holy. I realize this can be tough. Please do not think I am judging or condemning you, and don't heap condemnation on yourself. We are all sinners. This study helps us understand our calling to be set apart, holy, and dedicated to the Lord. It may be difficult, but we have Yeshua, who knows our weakness because He was tempted in every way (Heb. 4:15).

Skip to **1 Peter 1:22**. It says He purified our souls by our obedience to the truth (Word or Gospel). What will be the result?

_____

When we love others from our pure hearts, our conduct will change. We will treat others the way we want to be treated.

Please read **1 Peter 1:22-25**. How is the *Word* described in each of these verses?

_____

_____

Long after our flesh withers and dissolves into nothing but DNA, His Words remain. In what are you investing? *Something here for a little while or something that lasts forever?* His word is imperishable. God planted this seed in you and meant for it to grow and bear fruit. A tree grows from a single seed so it can produce fruit that carries a new seed to start a new life. We are to be like a tree (**Ps. 1**).

What does Psalm 1 say about the man who is like a tree?

_____

_____

Precious Living Stones

Turn to **1 Peter 2:1**. Because of the Word, what are we to get rid of?

_____

Please read **1 Peter 2:1-9**. Verse 4 says, *As you come to him a living stone, rejected by men but in the sight of God chosen and precious.* The world rejects us when God sets us apart. You are a living stone, precious and chosen by God; not one who is dead and useless. Even stones come to life when the Creator touches them. He gives LIFE to everyone who seeks and draws near to Him.
Verse 5 says we are living stones being built into something.

What are we being built into? _____

What will (your answer to above question) it *be*?

_____

What are we going *to do*?

_____

1 Peter 2:5 answers these questions. I have shown you how Yeshua is our Great High Priest, so this makes us His priesthood. What is our sacrifice? Turn to **Romans 12:1-2**. Keep your place in Peter though; we will be right back.

In **Romans 12:1**, what is the sacrifice we should offer?

_____

In the Old Testament, it was a living sacrifice God demanded. You could not come to the altar and bring a dead animal or even a sick one. It had to be perfect in every way. In the same sense, God wants our sacrifice to be living. We can't sacrifice something we consider dead or unwanted. Do you keep an idea alive in your heart, mind, and soul? Is there something you want? What do you hope for and dream of? Those are the things He wants. If it means a lot to you, then He wants you to surrender it to Him.
Is this easy? No. I have to do this daily. The most important wants and desires I have are those God

has for me. *Did you realize He has dreams for you?* When He created you, He put inside you the gifts and abilities to fulfill His dreams. Have you ever asked God for His vision for you?

In **Romans 12:1**, what other words describe this *living sacrifice*?

_____

We see the word *holy* here again. Before someone brought an animal in for sacrifice, it was washed. It had to be clean before offering it to God. We see this so much in God's Word. The priests had a ceremonial washing or bathing before they entered the Holy Place or the Most Holy Place. Baptism is a washing to symbolize being made clean. In **Exodus 19:10-11**, God told Moses to *consecrate* (or make holy) the people and have them *wash their clothes* to be ready for God's arrival on Mt. Sinai. Yeshua made us clean by taking away our sin with His blood.

I want to emphasize how God wants to set us apart, so we can dedicate our lives to Him every day. He wants us to seek Him, come to Him in prayer, and confess our sins and turn away from the ways of this world. If the world accepts you, chances are you will not be acceptable to God.

Please go back and reread **1 Peter 2:5-9**. We see in verse 5 that we, as living stones, are being built up as a spiritual house (meaning the Church) and within the Church, we are to be a holy priesthood. In verse 9, Peter refers to the Church as a *chosen race, a royal priesthood*, and a *holy nation*. This parallels what God considered Israel. I am not suggesting we have replaced Israel, as a few do. I am saying we are to be as God meant Israel to be if she were following Yeshua.

You see how Peter refers to us as a "holy priesthood" and a "royal priesthood"? As I stated earlier, God set the priests apart for His purpose and plan. This is how our lives are to be. We are to be "Holy to the Lord" as the priests of Israel were. We are to bless, offer prayers, ask the Lord for direction, and be servants of the Most High.

Sapphire - Day Four
Heaven, the priesthood, revelation, and *the Jehovah color*

The Perfect High Priest

Today, we are going to start reading **Hebrews 5:5-10**. As we see in verse 5, God appointed Yeshua as High Priest just as the high priests before Him. He did not exalt Himself even though He is the Son.

In verse 6, to whom is Yeshua compared?

_____

This verse comes from Psalm 110:4. However, we need to go back to Genesis to read about this man. Please turn to **Genesis 14:17-20**.

Let me summarize the story that leads up to these verses. Abram and his nephew, Lot had parted ways due to both men having so much stuff the land could not support all they had. Therefore, Abram, the generous and wise man he was, gave Lot first choice of the direction he went with his family, servants, flocks, and herds. Lot chose the Jordan Valley, with Sodom and Gomorrah, while Abram selected the land of Canaan. The people were wicked in the valley where Lot lived, and war broke out among the kingdoms south of Jerusalem (called Salem). The cowardly king of Sodom fled his country, and his enemies pillaged the city, snatching Lot as well. Abram heard of Lot's abduction, gathered his 318 men, pursued (and defeated) the men who had Lot, and took him home. Now, we've arrived at **Genesis 14:17**.

According to verse 18, Melchizedek has two titles. What are they?

_____

Melchizedek's name means "king of righteousness" (Heb. 7:2). He was a king and a priest. Do you see why Yeshua is a High Priest in the order of Melchizedek? He is not in *the order of* Levitical priests but the order of Melchizedek. No other priest in the Bible was both king and priest. That's not to say a king didn't try to do the job of the priest, but he was never both king and priest.

In 1 Peter 2, Peter referred to us as a "holy" and "royal" priesthood. I believe he was saying as followers and believers in Christ we shadow Yeshua's Royal and Holy Priesthood.

Please record what Melchizedek brings out to Abram in **Genesis 14:18**.

_____

Does this strike you as interesting? I believe it is a shadow of Yeshua's body and blood (**John 6:53-54**).

Returning to **Hebrews 5:6,** we read Yeshua is a priest *forever,* unlike any other priest. In **Hebrews 5:7-9**, we see Yeshua in a way Scripture rarely, if ever, showed any other priest. I love the first few words of verse 7, *In the days of his flesh...* Who else can this be said of in a literal sense? As you read verses 7-9, remember Yeshua is 100 percent man and 100 percent God; He is God in the flesh.

When He was in the flesh, how did Yeshua lift up prayers and supplications?

_____

Why was He heard?

_____

When we began this chapter, we read **Hebrews 4:16,** which told us we could approach the throne of grace with boldness. Boldness does not mean *without* reverence or godly fear. My husband and I taught our children they could come to us with any problem or question, even if they disagreed with us, if they did it with respect. This is the example we should follow when we come to our Father. I may not understand His answer or like His silence, but I can go to Him with my frustrations, fears, and even anger, as long as I do it with godly fear or respect. Yeshua knew this well. *He was heard because of his reverence* (Heb. 5:7). In His flesh (or humanity), He did not want to die; with loud cries and tears, He offered prayers to His Father. This makes Him a wonderful High Priest! He understands us.

According to **Hebrews 5:8-9**, what did Yeshua learn through His suffering?

_____

According to these same verses, what made Yeshua perfect?

_____

We saw this same wording in **Hebrews 2:10**. The Father made the Founder of our salvation perfect through suffering. I explained then and will repeat it now; perfect is a verb that means, *To be made complete*. It may be difficult to wrap our minds around the fact that God made Yeshua perfect through suffering so He could learn obedience. Even though He was God in the flesh, the Father did this to bring "many sons to glory." Yeshua went through this to stand in our place and be our righteous judge and High Priest.

In **Hebrews 5:9**, what did He become to us as He became perfection?

_____

_____

This verse ends with "to all that obey him." The word *obey* in this sentence means to listen. In the Hebrew and Greek languages, the act of hearing means obeying. This is not how our culture understands "hearing." We can "hear" our pastor, our teachers, or even the Holy Spirit, but God wants us to obey what we hear. Maybe the Holy Spirit has been speaking to you throughout this study.

Are you going to obey or just hear? Is there anything the Lord wants you to do that you may not be doing?

_____

_____

Sapphire – Day Five
Heaven, the priesthood, revelation, and *the Jehovah color*

We Must Not Become Lazy

Devotionals are an extremely popular way to have our "quiet time." There are also many great self-help books on the market. But we must be vigilant. It is quite easy to read a daily devotional instead of the Bible. Just because a book quotes scripture does not mean you are studying God's Word. God did not intend for His Word to be difficult to understand or intimidating. He wants us to take time to study the Bible to find the gems hidden within it.

Read **Hebrews 5:11-14**.

Why is the author of Hebrews rebuking his readers?

_____

_____

The Greek word for *dull* means to be slow, sluggish, or slothful. It refers to "a condition of spiritual apathy and laziness that prevents spiritual development."[5] The author wanted to go deeper, give them more insight on Yeshua as their High Priest, but he couldn't because of their spiritual laziness. This required new knowledge and understanding for them. Maybe it was too much work. Isn't that how we can feel, too?

Studying Scripture takes time and effort. God does not think less of us if we are not in His Word as much as He would like. He loves us no matter what. I do feel, however, it must sadden Him to see the time we invest in things that have no Heavenly value.

Do we need more teachers of the Word and evangelists going into our neighborhoods and workplaces? Yes. Do we spend too much time on our phones, iPads or binge watching our favorite shows on Netflix? Yes. Do we need to do better? Yes. Am I preaching to myself? Yes. The answer lies in putting those things aside for a set time and reading our Bibles to let the Holy Spirit guide us through the Word one verse at a time. Start with a few verses for five to ten minutes a day. Don't set unrealistic goals. Reading two or three verses to let God speak to you is better than reading one chapter or an entire book just so we can say we did it.

If you are a parent, can you imagine letting your ten or fifteen-year-old still drink from a sippy cup or a bottle for each meal? Unfortunately, that is the state of a lot of churches in our country.

Now, more than likely if you are doing this study, you want solid food. God's Word is multifaceted; it's meaningful and piercing. I have seen many Bible studies ask questions like, "What do you think this means?" or "How do you take this verse?" or "Chew on this." These studies never get to the meaning. If Bible study is just about what you think it means and how you want to apply it, then why do we need teachers and pastors? Hence, the problem. We do not hear to obey.

Please turn to and read **2 Timothy 4:2-3**. Mark this book; we will come back to it again...

What time is coming, according to these verses?

_____

I believe we are at that time. We live in a time when if you don't like what your Bible has to say, you can look for, and find, another one more palatable to your worldview.

In **Hebrews 5:13**, we see the result of wanting milk, not solid food.

What results when we live on milk?

_____

_____

Jump back over to **2 Timothy 3:16-17**. How does Scripture profit us?

_____

_____

Do you see the last thing listed in verse 16? What is it? In my version (ESV), it says, *training for righteousness*. The one who lives on milk is untrained or unskilled in the Word. As we have read in **Hebrews 2:1**, the author warned them against drifting away from what they have heard. In **Hebrews 3:12**, the author warned his audience against an evil, unbelieving heart to keep them from falling away. Drifting and falling away are dangerous places to be in for a follower of Yeshua. That begins the dullness of hearing.

According to **Hebrews 5:14**, what does solid food do for us?

_____

_____

Did you see how one was for the child and one for the mature? God doesn't want us to stop at knowing what Christ did for us and recognizing the power of the Gospel. (This is essential for the new believer.) He wants us to dig deep and see what He has for us as believers and followers of Yeshua. There is so much more to this life He has given us through His Son. He has riches and treasures for us in His Word.

Where was the sapphire? Did you see the beautiful blue hue in this chapter? Like the sapphire, we are being made into precious living stones chosen by God. He is building us up to be a royal priesthood with Yeshua as our Great High Priest. Draw near to His Throne with confidence. Let Him train you in righteousness through His Word, and it will be your treasure.

What did the Lord show or teach you in this chapter?

_____

_____

Are there any ways you feel the Lord wants to train you in righteousness?

_____

_____

The Word trains us in righteousness and we will grow in maturity. You will taste and know the Lord is good (Ps. 34:8).

Chapter 6 - Opal
The Promises of God

Day One

In 1936, an Australian found the now famous opal, Aurora Australis, named after the bright southern lights. He discovered the 180-carat stone six meters deep in a dried-up seabed with a starfish imprint on one side. Considered the world's most valuable opal, it has red, blue, and green colors against a black background. Worth over $750,000, the Australian sold it for just 100 pounds.[1]

The Hebrew meaning of the word *opal* is "precious stone."[2] The Romans thought the opal was the most precious stone because it possessed all the colors of the other gems.[3] Its iridescent colors symbolize "the promises of God."[4]

Hebrews chapter 6 continues the rebuke started in Hebrews 5:11. The message begun in the first ten verses of Hebrews 5 resumes in Hebrews 7, making Hebrews 5:11-6:20 a segue (segue-way) or transitional passage.

The author of Hebrews wanted to explain so much more about Yeshua's position and fulfillment of the royal priesthood but could not because of the lack of knowledge and understanding of the profound things of Scripture. In Hebrews 6, we will see this same concept repeated with encouragement added.

There is controversy surrounding the first six verses of Hebrews 6 whether eternal security exists. Many use these verses to argue once you have fallen away, as a true believer in Christ, it's impossible to come back to Yeshua. While others claim these verses are referring to people who only professed to be Christians, not true believers. In summary, there seem to be two camps: one, it's believed possible for a believer in Christ to lose their salvation by falling away; two, it's thought impossible to lose your salvation, because, if you slip away you were not saved in the first place.

I believe we need to look at the whole book of Hebrews as a complete letter instead of taking a few verses here and there to create an entire theology.

Let's review what we know about the book of Hebrews. First, Messianic Jews who were being persecuted by Jews are the audience. Having had everything taken from them and mistreated, many left their faith in Yeshua and returned to the Law, while others deserted their churches or stayed away from believers. (All of this will become plain as we read through Hebrews.)

In chapter 1, the author clarifies how Yeshua is better than angels because He is the Son. In chapter 2, He gives His **first warning** against neglecting our salvation or drifting away from the truth of Yeshua. He concludes with Yeshua's humanness and suffering to become the Founder of our Salvation.

Chapter 3 conveys Yeshua's superiority over Moses and reminds us of the Children of Israel's rebellion. The author also gives a **second warning** against unbelief, which results in falling away from their faith in Yeshua.

Chapter 4 continues the theme of unbelief and disobedience; reiterating how the Children of Israel hardened their hearts even though they heard God's Word. The author explains how God's words are life, producing action in us and through us, piercing between our soul and spirit to change us. The chapter closes showing Yeshua as our High Priest, who sympathizes with our weaknesses. Because this sinful world tempted Him in every way, we can approach the throne of grace with boldness.

Chapter 5 shows us Yeshua not only as our High Priest but as a royal High Priest in the order of Melchizedek. The author gives a **third rebuke** for failing to press into maturity by living on the milk of God's Word. To sum it all up, I believe the author is saying, "We have one awesome Savior! Why in the world aren't you seeking Him with everything you have?"

So, why aren't we seeking Him with everything we have? Is it because it may not be the most acceptable thing to do? Is it easier to keep our relationship with Yeshua quiet, so others don't make fun or reject us? What would you do if you were in the same situation as these Jewish Christians?

Record your thoughts.

_____

_____

_____

_____

Elementary Doctrine

Turn to **Hebrews 6:1-6**. Read this passage considering what we have read and learned so far. Try to silence any theology you may already have and read with an open mind.

What is *therefore* referring to in verse 1?

_____

The author begins this chapter by asking his readers to leave the "elementary doctrine of Christ."

What does he consider the "elementary doctrine of Christ?"

_____

_____

As you read, the author names six things he calls foundational in verses 1 and 2. He paired them into three groups united by a common thread. Remember, the author expresses these as foundational to faith, not something a mature believer needs to keep studying. He wants us to move on to the things of Yeshua that cause growth and maturity.

First, let's discuss *repentance from dead works* and *faith in God*. I enjoy how the New Living Translation interprets Scripture. Here is **Hebrews 6:1**:

So let us stop going over the basics of Christianity again and again. Let us go on instead and become mature in our understanding. Surely we don't need to start all over again with the importance of turning away from evil deeds and placing our faith in God.

This translation makes it clear what the author means. The first two doctrines deal with coming to Christ as a new believer. Once we have learned and understood these things and have put them into practice, we do not need to continue educating ourselves about them. *The Bible Exposition Commentary* refers to the "basics of Christianity" as the "ABCs of Christianity."[5]

Repentance and faith in God are fundamentals we share with brand new Christians and non-believers to help them develop a relationship with Yeshua. It begins their journey in the faith.

Also, the Greek word translated as *maturity* in this verse means *perfection*.[6] As we discussed in the last chapter, suffering perfected Yeshua. Since He is our example, wouldn't perfection be God's will for us as well? Milk does not fulfill perfection, solid food does. Holiness is a work of God that is solid food for us.

Verse 2 instructs us on washings and the laying on of hands. We examined washings as it pertains to holiness in the last chapter. Ceremonial washings were typical in the Jewish culture. These Jewish believers would have understood their meaning. Baptism is a ritual washing and is symbolic of new life in Christ. Many years ago, my youth pastor baptized me at fifteen years old. However, this past year while in Israel, my pastor baptized me in the Jordan River. Did I need to do it again? No. It was an emotional experience to be baptized in the same river as my Lord and re-affirm my faith in Him. No one needed to explain what we were doing and the meaning behind our action. Our group already had knowledge and maturity in this area.

The laying on of hands can have more than one purpose. In Acts 19:6, Paul used it as a conduit between himself and another to transfer gifts of the Holy Spirit. We also lay hands as we pray for healing or give blessings to a brother or sister in Christ (Jms. 5:14). Once again, we see this portrayed in the Old Testament when someone offered a sacrifice. The person presenting the lamb or goat as an atonement for their sin would push their hands down (as if to crush) on the animal's head as an act of transferring their sin onto the animal.

Please turn to **Isaiah 53:5, 10**. These verses describe what Yeshua went through for our iniquities or sin. Do you see the similarities between Yeshua and the laying of the hands on the animal sacrifice?

How is it described in **Isaiah 53:5 and 10**?

_____

_____

God transferred our sins to His Son so we would receive the blessings of eternal life. He crushed Him for us!

Opal – Day Two
The Promises of God

Giving Away vs. Losing

The last two doctrines mentioned in **Hebrews 6:2** are the *resurrection of the dead* and *eternal judgment*. Much is written on these in books and Bible studies. Most agree on the resurrection of the dead and eternal judgment.

Understanding resurrection and judgment is necessary because these two things lead to many interpretations and arguments. My husband often says, "I do not need to know, or care, how or when it will happen, as long as I go to Heaven." Reading and studying the books of Daniel and Revelation is an intriguing exploration of God's plan for this world. Unfortunately, I see too many pastors and Bible teachers resort to name calling and sarcasm toward those with differing beliefs. I wrote my first Bible study on Revelation; I love the book. That does not entitle me to belittle others for their understanding of these writings. Living a life worthy of eternal life is more important.

Hebrews 6:3 says, *And this we will do if God permits*. You need to go back to verse 1 to understand to what he is referring.

What will we do if God permits?

_____

There is more to God's Word than we understand. Start your prayers each day by asking God for the eyes of your heart to be enlightened and ask the Spirit to give you wisdom and revelation of the Father (Eph. 1:17-18). Desire relationship with the Father, Son, and the Holy Spirit, seek them with all your heart and pursue truth. If we are doing these things, then it is no longer about how many times we've prayed today or how much Scripture we've read and memorized—it becomes about Yeshua and how much we love Him. The outcome of your devotion to God will be growth and maturity.

Read **Hebrews 6:4-6**. These may be challenging verses to appreciate for most of us, including me. Let's ask the Holy Spirit to shed His light and truth on them.

Hebrews 6:4-6 begins with, *For it is impossible, in the case of those…* Write the four descriptions given of "those."

    1.

    2.

    3.

    4.

Let's examine each of these statements. First is written, *Those who have been enlightened*. The Greek word for *enlighten* means "to cause something to exist and thus come to light and become clear to all. To enlighten, spiritually, imbue with saving knowledge."[7] In this verse, the author refers to someone who has a saving understanding of the Gospel.

Second, it says, *those… who have tasted the heavenly gift and have shared in the Holy Spirit*. Here we see the Greek word for *tasted* is *experience*. These people have experienced the divine gift of salvation and the Holy Spirit.

Third, *they have tasted the goodness of the word of God and the powers of the age to come.* Everything listed in these two verses is describing someone who has experienced the Gospel firsthand, not merely professing a faith about which they know little. We can have head knowledge but no heart knowledge. Many can impress us with the multitude of Scriptures they have memorized, but there is little evidence those words have changed their lives and produced fruit. The author of Hebrews is not portraying these people. However, in verse 6, it says, *And then have fallen away.* The phrase *have fallen away*, means "to fall beside a person or thing, to slip aside. To deviate from the right path, turn aside, wander."[8]

I attended a church where I struggled with the theology they taught on this. At the time, I didn't know what I believed or what I should accept as true. As I prayed for understanding, the Lord used an analogy to help me: Imagine getting a pricy watch. First, you have the choice to take it or not, right? If you decide to accept the gift, there are two stipulations. The first one is, you must wear it and show it to everyone you know and meet every day. Second, you must tell them who gave it to you. Do you still want it? Suppose you tire of wearing this watch because it doesn't go with everything you have, or it isn't always proper to wear to the places you go. Eventually, it goes out of style. You get weary of talking about it because those around you don't want to know or hear about your watch. You decide you just can't live with those conditions anymore because it's hard and you are losing friends, so you return the gift. Did anyone take the present from you? Did you lose it? *No, you returned it.*

Every birthday and Christmas, I try to find my daughter gifts she will enjoy. She loves clothes and never has enough of them. (Sound familiar to anyone?) But, she is extremely picky, which is why she has too few clothes to wear. The time for opening her gifts comes; she looks at what I have given her and *seems* satisfied. Nevertheless, within days, she is returning most of what I gave her, or I find it a year later in a pile of clothes to give away *with the tags still on it*! Gifts get returned all the time. Besides Black Friday, one of the busiest retail shopping days is the day **after** Christmas. Have you ever been in the return or exchange lines at the mall?

Return to **Hebrews 6:6**. Verse 4 started out with *It is impossible...* The rest of that thought is in verse 6.

What is impossible according to **Hebrews 6:6**?

_____

According to this same verse, what is being done to the Son of God?

_____

The author of Hebrews says, *To their own harm...* Why is this to their harm? The Jewish New Testament Commentary raises a different point of view on these verses. Maybe this has nothing at all to do with Armenians and Calvinists. (Simplified, Armenians believe a believer can lose their salvation, while Calvinists think it is impossible). Remember, we are reading a book written to Messianic Jews who had grown up with the Law and practices of the Law. Imagine how hard it would be to stop all the sacrifices you had done since you can remember because Someone said: "It is finished!" The sacrifices they want to keep doing are like crucifying their Lord all over again. They cannot accept this truth, and it leads them to fall away. They have put their faith in animal sacrifices instead of the final sacrifice of the Lamb of God. As a result, they said Yeshua's sacrifice was not sufficient.

What has God done for you, but through your actions, you are in effect telling Him it is not good enough?

_____

_____

Forgiveness can be one of those things. You may have trouble forgiving yourself for something even though you asked and received forgiveness from the Father. When we continue in our unforgiveness, it is like telling God His mercy is not enough, we know better, and our judgment stands above His.

God has already given all He has to us for life and eternal life. When we ask for more of Him, He cannot give us more. What we need is to have less of ourselves so there is more room for Yeshua. John the Baptist said in John 3:30, *He must increase, but I must decrease*. There is only room enough for one of you or part of you. Most times, we are 75 percent us and 25 percent God, or even 50-50. God wants us to give Him more of ourselves so He can fill us with Himself.

Opal – Day Three
The Promises of God

Are you one of the few?

I grew up on a farm where we had a large garden our family worked in throughout the summer. I dreaded the weeding. Our parents sent my sisters and me out right after a rainstorm because the weeds came up easier. The thorny kinds were and still are the worst. But, if we had let them take over, the garden would have been unproductive. We could have missed out on the fruit it produced.

Today, we are starting with **Hebrews 6:7-8**. The author writes of a common practice during the time of Hebrews. When a field that produced a valuable crop became unusable by the thorns and weeds overtaking it, the farmer had to burn it to use it again. The rain, mentioned in this verse, represents God's blessings.

Re-read verses 7 and 8, but instead of the word *land* insert ***the heart***, and instead of the phrase *a crop* insert ***fruit***. How does it read now? Please write it here:

_____
_____
_____
_____

Do you see how this changes the verse? If we allow a weed or two (sin) to grow in our hearts, which Yeshua made pure, before long, sin overruns them. Let's look at some challenging verses. Please turn to **Matthew 7:21-22**.

According to these verses, who enters the Kingdom of Heaven?

_____

According to verse 22, who will say, *Lord, Lord, did we not prophesy in your name…*

_____

Notice, Yeshua does not say, "SOME will say, Lord, Lord..." or "A FEW will say, Lord, Lord..." He says, MANY. Why will God tell *many*, "I never knew you?" The answer is from **Matthew 7:21**, they have not done the will of the Father. The things listed in verse 22, prophesying, casting out demons, and mighty works all sound godly, but is it possible to do these things to glorify ourselves? In these verses, was God telling them to do these things or did they do them regardless of God's will for them?

Now, stay in Matthew 7, but consider verses 13 and 14.

How many find the narrow gate and the way that is hard?

_____

There may be people who think they are on the narrow path and may not be. I do not mean this to be judgmental or critical, but rather to caution us to examine ourselves and keep our hearts in line with the will of the Father.

What is the Father's Will?

What is the will of the Father? We could read verses about this all day. However, I will give you a few references, and let you write what the Father's will is according to that verse.

Luke 9:23.

_____

Ephesians 5:1-2.

_____

Colossians 1:9-10.

_____

_____

1 Thessalonians 4:1-5

_____

_____

God's greatest desire is for us to know His Son. Beyond that, abiding in Him and growing is essential. Let's look at each of your answers.

Luke 9:23. What does *deny yourself* mean, and how would you explain this to someone?

_____

_____

Here's what *Dictionary.com* says, "Deny oneself, to refrain from satisfying one's desires or needs; practice self-denial."[9] Who is most important to you? *God or yourself?* I am not suggesting anyone should become a monk. Denying yourself is between you and God. It's giving Him more rights to your plans, desires, and future than you have been giving.

Ephesians 5:1-2.
Imitate God by loving others. Let's face it; there are people we do not always get along with or even like. Some people have a way of getting under our skin or know how to push our buttons. However, loving others is God's will for us. God can do incredible things. Ask Him to fill you with His love for people, even those you may have a hard time loving.

Colossians 1:9-10.
Having spiritual wisdom is a mark of a mature believer, which leads to understanding and the knowledge of God. It is solid food. Are you walking in a manner worthy of your Savior? God wants us to bear fruit by doing the things He has called us to do. Let's explore this in **John 15:5**.

According to this verse, how do we bear fruit?

_____

1 Thessalonians 4:1-5.
Sanctification. There's that word again. How often do we hear about someone who is a virgin at the time of his or her marriage? Please don't misunderstand me. I am not trying to sound judgmental. I am referring to the world, not singling anyone out. But let's face it, being a virgin is not as common as it used to be.

Tim Tebow, the now-famous football player who would kneel and pray before every game, is open about abstinence. As a firm believer in Christ, his stand on waiting until marriage for sex has been made fun of by the media. It is out-of-style to be a virgin for any length of time, but it is in this way that God sets us apart.

A Just God

Now, for encouragement, please read **Hebrews 6:9-12**. The author begins by explaining his previous words (verses 4-6) were not about those to whom he is writing, because he says, ... *yet, in your case, beloved, we feel sure of better things...*

He is encouraging them to keep moving toward the better things of salvation.

In verse 10, how does the author describe God? _____

We might be tempted to think God is waiting for us to mess up so He can keep us out of Heaven. That could not be further from the truth. Do you realize how much God loves you? He wants us with Him for eternity. I believe He will do anything to get us. There is a song I adore called *Reckless Love* by Cory Asbury (Bethel Music).

This song is truth. Give God permission to light up your shadows, tear down the lies you believe, and kick down every wall you have erected. *For God is not unjust so as to overlook your work and the love you have shown for his name in serving the saints...* (Heb. 6:10). He notices everything we do and why we do it. He is not unjust, but just. What does *just* mean? Google says, "Based on or behaving according to what is morally right and fair."[10] God's nature will not allow Him to be anything but fair and righteous.

Opal – Day Four
The Promises of God

God's Promises

I saw a meme on Facebook with Yeshua holding a giant stuffed bear behind His back while holding out His hand, asking for the small bear in a child's arms. This spoke to me. I wonder how many times I have held on to something so dear to me, not realizing God had something even bigger in store for me. All He wanted was for me to give Him that small dream or possession I embraced.

Today, we will read about God's promises and His faithfulness to them.

Let's begin in **Hebrews 6:10.**

To what work is the author referring?

_____

_____

In verse 11, the author tells us to keep doing what we are doing.

What outcome, in verse 12, does he want us to avoid? _____

This word, used in verse 12, is the same Greek word referenced in **Hebrews 5:11**. How is it applied in that verse? _____

Instead of becoming lazy, what are we to do according to **Hebrews 6:12**?

_____

Who we are to imitate follows in **Hebrews 6:13-20,** and what they will inherit are promises. Notice in verse 12, the inheritance came through *faith* and *patience*. As I write this, I am reminded of specific promises God has given me that have not transpired. God is faithful! I must have faith and patience in what He has told me and keep pressing on and into Him.

What promises are you waiting on God to fulfill?

_____

_____

_____

References to Abraham (in Hebrews 6) and other Old Testament men of God (in Hebrews 11) is a reminder of their faithfulness to God's promises, many of which *were unfilled during their lifetime*. Readers of this letter were turning away from the faith and patience they once had. The author wants to encourage them to stay the course and not give up on their faith in Yeshua.

This message is still relevant to us today. I can get as discouraged, disappointed, and impatient as the next person. I'm sure you are no different. Don't give up and don't turn away from His love and promises. God loves us more than we know and together with His Son, and the Holy Spirit, They want to help, guide and teach us in every way. Trust Him to do what He says He will do.

Hebrews 6:13-14 refers to Genesis and God's promises to Abraham. Please turn back to a few of these passages with me to read the stories. First, read **Genesis 12:1-3**.

What promises does God make to Abraham in these verses?

_____

_____

At this point in Scripture, Abraham's wife, Sarah could not conceive, and Abraham was at least seventy-five years old. Put yourself in their place. How would you react? Now, please read **Genesis 17:15-19**.

What promises does God vow Abraham in these verses?

_____

_____

What is Abraham's reaction in verse 17?

_____

Have you ever laughed out loud at an impossible thing God said or showed you? God wanted to show Abraham and Sarah who He was. When they were at the end of themselves and nothing they tried worked, God said, "I AM!" He is still showing Himself as I AM today. He is the answer to every question, problem, or trial we are facing.

Go to **Genesis 22:6-18**. It's more to read, but worth it. In this story, we see a father giving his son as a sacrifice. In verse 7, Isaac saw the wood and fire but no lamb for the burnt offering. From Abraham's reply in verse 8, we see he may have suspected God's intervention. Regardless, he was obedient to God and willing to kill his son as a sacrifice. What obedience! He was ready to give the only son he and Sarah had waited for decades to have. In Genesis 22:1-4, when God told Abraham to offer his son as a sacrifice Abraham had no reply, argument, or tantrum. He went where God told him.

This kind of obedience is hard, but God wants it from us. No argument, deal making, debating, or tantrum; just do what He asks. Read verses 16-18 again.

What is God's reaction to what Abraham did?

_____

_____

God did not want Abraham to kill his son, but if he had, God could resurrect him. God planned to give His Son, so Abraham did not have to. The Father may never ask us to offer Him our only child, but He asks us to surrender precious things to Him.

A Lesson from my ducks

I have the cutest ducks. Real ducks that wobble, quack, and sometimes honk at me. I was complaining to the Lord one day. I had bought them to be my pets. Yes, the eggs are great, but I thought they would be a cute addition to our pond. However, they are timid, afraid for me to get close, and if I try to give them peas, which they love, they won't take them until I back away. They don't trust me. I had a nice-sized enclosure and baby pool for them while they were young. When they got bigger, I wanted to introduce them to the rest of our property and the big pond we have. They did not want to leave the small enclosure and baby pool. When I finished telling this to the Lord, He said, "Welcome to *My* world." I laughed as I considered that.

We are no different from my ducks. God bought us with the blood of His Son to restore relationship with us, but we struggle to trust Him. Our fear of Him or His plans keep us at a distance. He has a massive world for us with a giant pond to play in, but we want to stay in our little pool with our comfortable surroundings. Take a chance. Ask Him what big things He wants to show you and where you are settling for less. Get out of the baby pool!

Turn back to **Hebrews 6:13** with me. A promise is a great thing, but people do not always keep them. We may lump God in the same heap of people who have not honored their promises. But God does not base His promises on who we are, who we have been, or who we will be; He bases his promises on WHO HE IS!

The Bible is full of God's promises. We may not always recognize them, but they are there. Turn with me to a few verses and record the promise you read. I hope at least one of these speaks to you today.

Exodus 14:14

_____

Isaiah 41:10

_____

_____

Isaiah 54:10

_____

_____

Deuteronomy 31:8

_____

Psalm 37:4

_____

Revelation 3:5

_____

Disappointment and discouragement have caused many to turn from God. We may think God has not heard us, was not there during a difficult time, or has not helped us in the way we needed. God's time is not our time, and God's ways are not our ways. His timing and methods are perfect, and we cannot understand until He shows it to us. That is why it is possible to fall away when we have tasted the goodness of God.

Opal – Day Five
The Promises of God

Heirs to the promise

In the last chapter, we read about the ephod and the twelve stones, which were a remembrance before God. What command did Yeshua give regarding communion? *Do this… in remembrance of me* (1 Cor. 11:25). God and His Son want us to remind them. Don't misunderstand what I am saying, *they* do not forget. We are the ones who forget what God has done for us. Just consider the Children of Israel. How many of us have criticized them by thinking, "If God went before me in a cloud by day, and a pillar of fire by night, parted the Red Sea, fed me with manna on the ground, and performed miracles, I could never doubt as they did." How we forget.

God wanted Aaron to remind Him of His promises every time he or the other priests stepped into the Holy Place. The Israelites tested Him, angered Him, turned to heathen gods, made Him jealous, disobeyed Him, and cursed Him, among other things. Wouldn't you need to recall the promises you gave if someone treated you this way? Are we unlike the Israelites? Were Abraham, Isaac, Jacob, or David without sin? Did God keep His promises to them? YES. He did it for HIS name, not because they were perfect or even good. He does it because HE is GOOD!

Hebrews 6 ends with words of encouragement for us. Let's look at God's character in these last eight verses.

In **Hebrews 6:13**, who does God swear by? _____

According to **Hebrews 6:15** when did Abraham get the promise God had made to him?

_____

Who wants to wait, right? It is hard to wait. I must admit, I am impatient, but I pray for more tolerance. Fortunately, we serve a God who is long-suffering. Can you imagine the consequences if He weren't? What if God had given up on you the first time you blew it? Suppose if God had as little patience as you or me. I would be in trouble.

Hebrews 6:16, reads like a judge giving instructions to a witness. Before taking the stand, they must swear, "So help me God," as an oath to tell the truth. Verse **17** tells us God did the same thing. When He made an oath to the *heirs of the promise* He had no one higher to swear by, so He swore by Himself (verse 13).

Who are the "heirs to the promise?"

_____

What did God show to the "heirs of the promise?"

_____

Unchangeable

The author starts verse **18** by saying, *So that by two unchangeable things, in which it is impossible for God to lie…*

What are the two unchangeable things?

It is IMPOSSIBLE for God to lie. Do you believe it?

Please read **Numbers 23:19** and **Titus 1:2**. What do these verses tell you concerning God?

God is not just truthful—He is Truth. There is a distinction. We lie, God CAN NOT. These are absolutes used by Scripture to describe God's nature. It's hard to trust people after they've lied to you. Even though God cannot lie and never has, we still find it hard to be secure in what He says. I discovered I have a hard time trusting people even though they have never wronged me.

One day while driving, God spoke to my heart and told me why I don't trust. He showed me the first person I could not depend on and the impact it has had on my life. I needed God to heal that young woman (in me) who had learned not to rely on others.

Do you know anyone unchangeable? People change their minds like they change their clothes. Hurt and betrayal make us into a different person. Education or success may transform us. We may even alter our opinions, good or indifferent, regarding the people in our lives. Thank God, *He is* unchangeable! His mind does not vary toward you or me. He loves us even though we fall, walk away, or deny His existence. The only way He loves us more is when we worship His Son!

Verse **18** says, ... *we who have fled for refuge...* Turn to **Joshua 20:1-6**. God directed His people to appoint cities for refuge. Anyone who killed another by accident could go to these towns for protection from the avenger of blood, or kinsmen-redeemer. The manslayer had to stay in the city of refuge until the high priest died, and then he could return to Israel.

A kinsman-redeemer was a male relative responsible for taking care of and protecting a family. The story of Ruth shows how Boaz took care of and married Ruth as her kinsman-redeemer. He is a shadow of Yeshua.

In **Genesis 4:8-16**, we read the story of Cain and Abel. God asked Cain, *Where is Abel, your brother?* Cain denies knowing his whereabouts, but God said, *The voice of your brother's blood is crying to me from the ground.* This story shows how God is the avenger of blood. He punished Cain by driving him away from everything he knew.

Returning to **Hebrews 6:18**, Yeshua is that city of refuge for us. In a way, God is the avenger of blood. Before Yeshua came, God needed a blood sacrifice to atone for the unintentional sins people committed against Him (Lev. 4:1, 13, 22, and 27). After Yeshua's death and resurrection, God finished avenging. Our High Priest will never die, so we will never have to leave the city of refuge.

According to **Hebrews 6:18**, what do these unchangeable things give us?

Our Anchor

Please read **Hebrews 6:19-20**.

What is our anchor, according to these verses?

An anchor is a weight that keeps the ship from drifting away with a current of water. Hope is the anchor that keeps us from drifting away from God. Think what it means to be hopeless.

I home-schooled my children up to their senior year of high school, then allowed them to choose what they wanted to do during their last year. My daughter spent it at our public school. She thought she would love it. Although there were ways in which she liked going off to her classes every morning and meeting other people, there were ways she disliked it as well.

My daughter's gift is discernment. She can see or sense things concerning people they may be unaware they are showing. One day as we were discussing her day at school, she said, "The people in this school have no hope." I could tell it made her sad. She had a sense there was nothing in their lives in which they could place their trust or hope. She asked me, "How can people go on with their lives without God?"

Our hope is in Yeshua. It is *a hope that enters into the inner place behind the curtain* (Heb. 6:19). Within the Temple, there was a Holy Place and the Holy of Holies with a curtain between them. Only the high priest could enter the Holy of Holies once a year. Yeshua was broken, and the veil torn in two, top to bottom to open the way into the Holy of Holies for us. He entered that place before us, becoming our forerunner.

Everything we have discussed in this chapter, from the elementary doctrine, the falling away of those who have tasted the word of the Lord's goodness, the heart set on fire to rid it of thorns and thistles, led to the unchangeable promises, oaths, and truths of God. Yeshua is our King and High Priest who stands in royal authority mediating between God and man.

What better hope do we have? *A God who keeps His promise never to let us go.*

Where was the opal in this chapter? Where did you find promises of God?

_____

_____

As we read in the last chapter, Peter wrote we are God's precious, living stones, similar to the Hebrew meaning for opal. In Hebrews 6, we see our God is a keeper of His promises. He cannot lie, and He will not change His mind regarding us. His nature allows us to trust Him with everything.

Chapter 7 – Hope Diamond
Hope that comes from Yeshua

Day One

The Hope Diamond is the most infamous gem ever. This jewel has many myths and legends associated with it. Named after Henry Philip Hope, this rock is a whopping 45.52 carats, with a blue hue from the mineral boron. Sixteen white diamonds surround it, while a forty-five-diamond chain holds this astonishing pendant.[1]

A wealthy, young heiress, Evalyn Walsh McLean, was the last private owner of this magnificent necklace. The daughter of an Irish immigrant, who struck it rich in the gold rush, bought the gemstone for $180,000. As a socialite, everyone knew her for her extravagant parties, but she was no stranger to loss. Her oldest son died in a car accident, her daughter overdosed on sleeping pills, and her husband left her for another woman. She died with many debts, and her estate sold the jewels to cover those bills.[2] The Smithsonian Natural History Museum displays the Hope diamond now.

Even owning the famous Hope diamond was not enough to give Evalyn Walsh McLean what she needed. She lost so much during her lifetime. Gems like hers are temporary. Our real treasure is the hope that comes from Yeshua.

Yeshua's hope

Life happens. Many people say this phrase. I don't believe everything is a coincidence. Most things happen for a reason: the people we meet, the job we land, or even a move to a new place. Relationship loss, betrayal, and death occur because we live in a fallen world where Satan has power, for now. Understanding why difficult or even horrible things transpire in our lives and why we lose those we love can be tough. Time, the Holy Spirit, and the love of others will get us through the challenges this life throws at us.

Through our trials, we have a Father and Savior who stick by our side. Yeshua came to be hope in our darkest, most difficult times. At the end of Chapter 6, we read we have no better hope. Even when we are unaware, it is a sure and steadfast anchor.

We will learn why Yeshua is our better hope. Hebrews 7 reintroduces the comparison of Yeshua and Melchizedek by picking up where Hebrews 5:1-10 left off. It may help to reread those verses. In Chapter 5 of this study, I gave you a summary of how Abram met Melchizedek and explained his name. We will revisit that.

The author of Hebrews wants to make an essential parallel between Yeshua and Melchizedek and the fact Yeshua is a priest in the order of Melchizedek. We will discover how Melchizedek's interaction with Abram is significant, too. You may wonder how this applies to our daily lives and relationship with Yeshua. We have to believe it does because the author kept coming back to Yeshua and Melchizedek. His audience frustrated the author since he could not go deeper into these things because they were *dull of hearing* (Heb. 5:11). I intend to unpack this chapter and help you realize why it is imperative to understand.

Let's set the stage before we continue. **Genesis 14** recounts the story of four Mesopotamian tyrants who sought to control the region of five rebellious Canaanite kings. A battle ensued, and when the Mesopotamian kings overtook Sodom and Gomorrah, they took their possessions and provisions, along with Lot and his wealth. After finding out about this by one who escaped, Abram and his small army of 318 men went after Lot and the others taken. Please understand, the five Canaanite kings could not do what Abram and his 318 men did. He defeated the four tyrants, brought back not only Lot and his possessions, but also the other captives and their goods.

In **Hebrews 7:1-10**, we will explore Melchizedek, his priesthood, and Abram's encounter with him. We will also compare his priesthood with that of Aaron and the Levitical priests.

Please read **Hebrews 7:1**.

When does Melchizedek meet Abram?

_____

In this verse and the one found in Genesis 14:18, Melchizedek is a priest of the *Most High God*. This name is his Hebrew title *El Elyon,* and the first appearance of this name is in **Genesis 14:17-22**. Let's turn there and read those verses.

In these six verses, we see the name *God Most High* used four times. El is the Hebrew name for God, and Elyon comes from an adjective meaning *high*. Strong's defines it as "a title for the true God with a focus on him being supreme and shows high status".[3] In Genesis 14:19-20, Melchizedek blesses Abram by this same name and exalts God for delivering Abram's enemies into his hands.

In **Genesis 14:22**, Abram uses the word LORD before God Most High. LORD is the Hebrew word Jehovah or Yahweh. As we mentioned in Chapter 3, Jehovah means "he is everything and everything we need."[4] He is I AM.

Abram uses a third description of God (as does Melchizedek earlier) in that same sentence. What is it? _____

Abram not only recognized who God Most High is, but he included in his oath God is Everything and Creator of everything. After this, in Genesis 15, God makes a covenant with Abram and promises him an heir. When Abram had no hope of ever having an heir, God provided. God is good. The Lord gave victory to Abram over his enemies, blessings by Melchizedek, and a promise for an incredible reward.

To tithe or not to tithe

Look again in Hebrews 7. God arranged a meeting between two men to show Abram a type or shadow of His own Son. **Hebrews 7:2** tells us how Abram responded to Melchizedek.

What did Abram give Melchizedek?

Tithing is an ancient practice, and I realize there are different beliefs about it. I am not interested in tackling that in this study. However, my husband and I tithe to our church and give offerings and gifts for situations. Bottom line, we contribute as the Lord directs us.

My family lost our sweet German shepherd, Olivia, to a terrible accident. It was January, and we had weeks of single-digit temperatures, which froze our pond. However, we had two warmer days, and on this day it was sixty degrees. Olivia had gone onto the pond and fallen through the melting ice in the center. We were not home and because of the ice around the perimeter, she could not get out of the still-freezing water. When we got out of the car, only one of our two dogs came to greet us. After calling and looki.ng for her, my husband found her floating in a small area of water. We were in disbelief and utterly devastated. I realize she was a dog, but she was part of our family. We loved her and still miss her. I grieved over this dog and didn't understand why the Lord let her die the way she did. The Lord showed me He understood my pain and loss. He reminded me of the verse that says, *Are not two sparrows sold for a penny? Yet not one of them will fall to the ground outside your Father's care* (Matt

10:29 NIV). He knew what would happen to Olivia, and I can only hope it happened quickly.

One day two weeks later, the Holy Spirit impressed upon me if I believe everything I have is His, then Olivia was His to take. I realize if you have lost a spouse or child these are difficult words to read. However, the Lord was not unkind when He spoke them to my heart. It comforted me. Everything I have, from my family to my house and property, belongs to Him. I can trust Him with it, too.

Because of this, we don't stop at 10 percent but see this as a starting point.

Hope Diamond - Day Two
Hope that comes from Yeshua

I heard from one of our church board members if every Christian church member tithed, the Church would collect $200,000,000,000, which is $200 BILLION. The UN predicts it takes $30 billion a year to end world hunger.[5] The Church could help end world hunger if we were all faithful in giving.

Hebrews 7:2 says Abram gave a tenth of everything he had to Melchizedek from his victory over the Mesopotamian kings. *Why?* He recognized Melchizedek's greatness.

Read **Hebrews 7:2-3**.

What do these verses say about Melchizedek?

_____

_____

_____

Read verse 4, please.

It says, *See how great this man was to whom Abraham the patriarch gave a tenth of the spoils!* (Italics mine). Do you see how remarkable Melchizedek was? Do you understand why the author of Hebrews refers to Abraham, the patriarch, instead of Abram?

Abraham, whose name God changed after His covenant, was a great man then and now to all Bible-believing Christians and Jews alike. The Bible says if we are in Christ then Abraham is our father, too (Gal. 3:7-9). If Abraham gave a tenth of his spoils to a great man who *resembled* the Son of God, how much more should we give *to the Son of God*? Isn't Yeshua greater than Melchizedek or Abraham?

I don't believe because we give God our tithes and offerings, we will get monetary blessings in return. He blesses our obedience. The Bible says God loves a cheerful giver. We give to God because He is good, but also because HE is GOD. We commit to God out of what He has given us. All we have is His, because He has given us everything.

Obviously, Melchizedek is not the Son of God. But because there is no record of his mother, father, birth, death, or any successor, Melchizedek's priesthood continues forever. In this way, he resembles the Son of God. Yeshua does not resemble him. The focus of this passage is Yeshua's Priesthood and Kingship rather than Melchizedek's.

Family trees and tribes

Next, let's examine **Hebrews 7:5-10**. If you recall, the Levites were the tribe that included Aaron, Moses' brother. They were the priests of God.

What are the Levites commanded to do, according to verse 5?

_____

Turn to **Numbers 18:21-24** with me. Why are the Levites to receive a tithe?

_____

Read verse 24 in the same passage. What is the tithe according to this verse?

_____

Our pastors and other staff of our church are serving much as the Levites did during the time of Moses in the tent of meeting or tabernacle. Like the Levites, pastors, worship leaders, and teachers serve the church. When we give our tithes and offerings to God, they go toward paying our pastors and staff just as in biblical times.

In **Hebrews 7:5**, from whom have the Levites descended?

_____

If you have read much of the Bible, you may have skimmed past a few genealogies. Genesis, 1 Chronicles, Matthew, and Luke have significant family trees going back to Adam. Even Paul lets us know his lineage in the books he wrote. It was essential to the Jewish people during the time of the Bible that they knew from whom they descended and to what tribe they belonged. This is clear in Hebrews. Scripture tells us Melchizedek did not descend from the Levites, so he did not function under the same commandment in Numbers 18.

So now, let's look at **Hebrews 7:6-7**. The phrase "this man" is referring to Melchizedek. It says he received tithes from Abraham. Now, I will give you a short grammar lesson. It is essential to understand this word as it pertains to this passage. The word *received* is an active, perfect tense word. Those of you who love English know what I'm talking about.

The *Glossary of Morpho-Syntactic Database Terminology* defines perfect tense in this way: "Perfect — The verb tense used by the writer to describe a completed verbal action that **occurred in the past** but which produced a state of being or a result that **exists in the present** (in relation to the writer). *The emphasis of the perfect is not the past action so much as it is as such but the present 'state of affairs' resulting from the past action.*"[6] (Emphasis mine) This definition is saying the perfect tense describes something that happened in the past, but because of the action, it continues into the present.

What does this passage mean to us? Melchizedek received tithes from Abram in the past, but according to the verb tense, the receiving of the tithe continues into the present.

Verse 7 shows us another point.

Who is the inferior and who is the superior?

_____

Since an Orthodox Jew would argue the superiority of the Levitical priesthood to any other, the author includes verse 7. He is making the point that for Abraham to have given Melchizedek a tithe could only show the supremacy of this priest to Abraham.

Let's look at **Hebrews 7:8**. I hope this will help you understand the point I am trying to make. The writer of Hebrews gives us two cases.

Who are the mortal men in the first case? _____

In the next case, who is still living?

_____

If you answered Yeshua or Melchizedek for the last question, you would be right. *Why?* I said earlier Melchizedek had no successor according to the Bible, so that makes him a priest forever. In this way, he lives forever. That's why Yeshua is a priest in the order of Melchizedek; he is a High Priest forever. So, when Abraham gave tithes to Melchizedek, it was as though he was giving to the Son of God and set in motion the act of giving and receiving of tithes continuing to the present time.

Let's read **Hebrews 7:9-10**. In these verses, the author is having fun at the Levites' expense.

How were the Levites paying tithes to Melchizedek and, in a way, to the Messiah?

_____

_____

The phrase the author begins verse 9 with is a phrase not found anywhere else in the Bible. He wants his readers to see the superiority of Melchizedek to Abraham and the Levites who were still to descend from Abraham.

Hope Diamond - Day Three
Hope that comes from Yeshua

Perfection from the Perfect

In **Hebrews 7:11-28**, we will see the comparison of Yeshua and Melchizedek with the focus on Yeshua's priesthood and perfection.

There were about 430 years between Abraham and the time when Moses began the Levitical priesthood. Melchizedek was the first priest of the Most High God we see in Scripture. There were no other priests mentioned until Moses received the Torah and established the Tent of Meeting and the Levitical priesthood.

Please read **Hebrews 7:11-14**. In verse 11, the word *perfection* is the Greek word *teleiosis*, which means "fulfillment or completion."[7] The *Jewish New Testament Commentary* defines *teleiosis* as "reaching the goal."[8]

Why wasn't perfection attainable through the Levitical priesthood?

_____
_____

In verses 1 through 10, our author built a case for the superiority of Melchizedek. However, in verse 12 he states if the priesthood changes, then the Law must change. In verses 13 and 14, the author tells us why.

Aaron and his descendants came from which tribe? _____

Yeshua came from which tribe? _____

Had a priest ever come from the same tribe as Yeshua? _____

The writer wants his readers to understand the Levitical priesthood was imperfect and just practice for the real priesthood. To the Jews of His day, Yeshua was threatening the one thing on which they depended and identified: their Law. Turn to **Matthew 5:17**.

According to this verse, what did Yeshua come to do?

_____

We must understand why God gave the Torah to His people. It was always to point out their need for perfection and their inability to achieve it. There was not a single Levitical priest who could attain perfection on his own or give it to someone through a sacrifice. Perfection can only come from one who is perfect. Yeshua is perfect.

In **Matthew 5:17**, the word *abolish* means "to tear down, destroy, or put an end to,"[9] while the word *fulfill* means "to satisfy, make complete, or finish."[10] Yeshua never came to destroy the Law as some teachers or scholars might have us think. The Law serves a godly purpose to point to Yeshua. He still uses it today to lead the Jews to Yeshua. Most Messianic Jews live by the Torah by keeping the Feasts, the Sabbath, and most dietary laws. The Law was for them. They were/are to be a light to the world and draw Gentiles to the one true God.

Let's dig into the book of Acts.

In **Acts 15**, the Jerusalem council debated what to do with Gentiles coming to Yeshua and how they should keep the Law. **Acts 15:10-29** tells us since they could not expect the Gentiles to observe all the Law, they decided what parts of the Law they needed to follow. Read **Acts 15:10-29** and pay particular attention to verse 19.

From what four things are the Gentiles to abstain?

_____

_____

These four things were a way we, as Gentiles, could keep the fundamental rules of the Torah. It satisfied the Law of God and Moses in the eyes of the Jews.

Please read **Hebrews 7:14-17**. Verses 14 and 15 start with similar phrases such as, *It is clear* or *It is evident…*

What becomes even clearer regarding the priesthood?

_____

Depending on which version of the Bible you are reading, verse 15 uses the word *another* as in … *when another priest* arises… The New Living Translation is more correct in its interpretation: *The change in God's law is even more evident from the fact that a different priest who is like Melchizedek, has now come.*

The word *another* comes from the Greek word *heteros* where we get the English prefix *hetero* (like heterosexual), meaning different.[11] This different priest is Yeshua. He was not just another priest, but a different one coming from a unique order.

Hebrews 7:16 tells us the basis of Yeshua *rising* as our Priest. What is it?

_____

The Greek word for *arises* means, "jump up, spring up to one's feet."[12] Isn't that what Yeshua did when He rose from the dead? According to *The Bible Sense Lexicon*, indestructible means, "impossible to be destroyed or undone; consequently, continuing or existing forever."[13]

Please turn to **John 10:17-18**.

What do these verses say about Yeshua's authority?

_____

NO ONE killed Yeshua. Nothing could destroy Him. He gave His life for us. Yeshua chose to die. He laid down His life and picked it up. As hard as it is to understand, Yeshua raised Himself from the dead because His life is indestructible.

In **Hebrews 7:17**, who said, *You are a priest forever, after the order of Melchizedek?*

_____

Turn to **Luke 3:21-22**. Who is speaking, and what do they say about Yeshua?

_____

_____

When God declares something about us or over us, it is *true*. Period. When Satan assigns something to us or over us, it is a lie. ***Who are you going to believe?*** Does anyone want to continue living a defeated, depressed, and condemned life? We can exchange all of those lies for a life based on who God says we are.

He says He loves us.

He declares we are His children.

Here is **Romans 8:38-39** in the NLT:

And I am convinced that nothing can ever separate us from his love. Death can't, and life can't. The angels can't, and the demons can't. Our fears for today, our worries about tomorrow, and even the powers of hell can't keep God's love away. Whether we are high above the sky or in the deepest ocean, nothing in all creation will ever be able to separate us from the love of God that is revealed in Christ Jesus our Lord.

Here are a few "can't (s)" we could add to this verse: Addiction can't, rejection can't, and our shame can't separate us from God's love. Child of God, what struggle has you convinced God can't love you through it? Like Paul, write it down and say it out loud.

Declare and BELIEVE "it" can't keep you from the love of God!

_____

_____

_____

Hope Diamond - Day Four
Hope that comes from Yeshua

While I wrote this study, one of my sisters read and worked through it. She is a retired schoolteacher and lives in another state. We don't get to visit often, but through technology, we talk and see each other as often as we want.

After she finished the first six chapters of this study, I received a text from her asking me to pray for her. She said it was nothing bad, but she had something she needed to talk to me about but was too emotional to talk at that point. Later, through tears of joy she told me how she had experienced God in a new way. He was next to her as she prayed words she couldn't in the past. As a result of pursuing God with all her heart, total honesty, and surrendering to Him, God healed her. For twenty years, my sister secretly struggled with alcohol. She has health problems because of it and always felt rejected and condemned by God because she could not control her drinking problem.

That day, God showed her He cared about her problems, her health, and her insecurities. He revealed He had NEVER rejected or condemned her despite her addiction. God set her free! For the first time in her life, she experienced complete love, acceptance, and hope from her Savior.

A Better Hope

Now let's look at **Hebrews 7:18-19**. In these verses, we see two opposing sides of an argument by the use of *on the one hand*. The first side is about the *former commandment*, which refers to **Hebrews 7:14-16**.

What commandment, regarding the priesthood, is the author referring to?

_____

_____

The phrase *set aside* comes from the Greek word meaning annulment, denoting "the act of officially or legally canceling something."[14]

Why was this commandment annulled?

_____

_____

Do not think the author is annulling the whole Torah along with this commandment. What does he say about the Law in verse 19?

_____

The only one who can make anyone perfect is Yeshua. Because of His suffering and indestructible life, He is the only perfect Priest and our only way to attain life.

Next, the author says, *But on the other hand…*

What *better hope* was introduced? (Note this is not a *who*, but a *what*. Refer to Hebrews 6:18-20, 7:17). The rest of verse 19 says, *Through which, we draw near to God.*

_____

_____

This is the hope I was referring to when we began this chapter. Yeshua gives hope to the discouraged, depressed, grieving, frightened, or lonely. It's the confidence that tells us this is not the end; this is not all there is to life. There is so much more. Yeshua gives us hope because He took our punishment and shed His blood. The hope we have through Him is better than the hope through the Law; it draws us near to God. They could not approach the Throne of God under the Law; no one could even go into the Holy of Holies unless they were the high priest. We have a better hope.

A Better Covenant

Please read **Hebrews 7:20-22**. Verse 20 starts with, *And it was not without an oath…*

What is the "it" in that sentence?

_____

The Levites became priests because their fathers were. Becoming a priest required consecration, but not an oath.
Verses 21 and 22 refer to Yeshua.

Who made the oath?

_____

What is the oath?

_____

_____

What makes Yeshua the guarantor (guarantee) of a better covenant?

_____

_____

A guarantor is "a person of sufficient means who *offers his* belongings, freedom, or often *his life* as an assurance that another person will meet certain specifications or requirements; especially in a financial context of debt repayment."[15] (Emphasis mine).
Pause here and let the meaning of this word and the context of Hebrews 7:22 sink in. What a great word to describe Yeshua. He has sufficient means, right? Yeshua owns everything and offered His freedom and life as our assurance. The difference is, He did it all and paid our debt.
We will unpack the new or better covenant in Hebrews 8, but for now, we will move on.
Continue by reading **Hebrews 7:23-25**. Verse 23 refers to Hebrews 7:18-19 and gives a reason the former commandment was weak and useless.

What is one reason?

_____

_____

In verse 24, this man, or "he" is Yeshua. What makes His priesthood different?

_____

The priesthood was to be ongoing and forever, but the Levitical priest could not. They, like us, lived in mortal tents. We needed one priest who could continue this priesthood forever. What God started in the Torah was good. However, because mortal man carried it out, it was not perfect. Only One who is perfect could make what God designed perfect.

Since Yeshua's priesthood is permanent and continues forever, what can He do the Levitical priest could not? _____

The word for *save* in this verse is *sozo*. We first talked about it in Chapter 1. The next word is *uttermost*. It means "all complete, perfect."[16] Yeshua can restore, heal, deliver, and preserve us completely. We can receive healing for all our needs whether they are emotional, spiritual, or physical. I know there are many views on healing and there have been abuses within the Church. However, *sozo* takes on a different connotation than we realize. Pray and ask the One who is faithful and true to reveal how He wants to heal you. Don't let unbelief keep you from what God has for you. Believe and receive, because Yeshua cares for and loves you.

Write any verses that come to mind or any words the Holy Spirit speaks to your heart.

_____
_____
_____
_____

Hope Diamond - Day Five
Hope that comes from Yeshua

You may have heard it said about someone, "He lives and breathes basketball," or "She lives to make music," or name your passion. Sports, a musical instrument, or subject may be our thing, but it is not our identity. Being a teacher is what I love to do, but it does not define who I am. I am a child of God. He wants to be our only obsession and stronghold.

Notice at the end of verse 25, what does Yeshua *live* to do?

_____

Who are the "them" in verse 25?

_____

Intercession means "to plead, appeal for, and petition."[17] We intercede for our sick, unsaved, or troubled loved ones to our Heavenly Father. But Yeshua lives for this! Notice the condition written into this verse. Yeshua wants us to draw near (approach, come near, seek association with, to join with, or agree with[18]) to God through Him. He is the only priest we need. Yeshua is the priest who intercedes for us *as we seek God.*

Turn to **Jeremiah 29:11-13**. If you have been in church for a while, you may have heard Jeremiah 29:11. Make a note of the conditions when you read the rest of these verses.

Starting in **Jeremiah 29:12-13**, what does God want us to do?

_____

_____

As a result, what does God promise?

_____

God doesn't just say, "Seek me." How does He want us to seek Him?

_____

We have sayings like, "Put your heart into it" or "I poured my heart out" and even, "My heart wasn't in it." If you have ever said one of these phrases, you appreciate what God wants. Our heart breaks when we pour into someone who doesn't return our feelings; but it is how we are to seek God. However, God will not disappoint or break our hearts. We can trust Him because He loves us so much!

Men often gift heart-shaped pendants as a sentimental keepsake. It requires enormous skill to cut and maintain the brilliance of the heart-shaped stone.[19] God is our Master Jeweler. He alone has the skills and tools it takes to make our hearts sparkle.

Read the final verses of Hebrews 7.

In **Hebrews 7:26**, what are the characteristics of our High Priest?

_____

_____

Think on these five things. Write out the meanings of these words. Compare the words from different versions of the Bible, too, if you can.

_____

_____

_____

_____

_____

For the last two verses, use the chart below. Contrast Yeshua to the Levitical priest from **Hebrews 7:27-28**. I have done a few for you.

Yeshua	Levitical priests
	Daily sacrifices
Appointed by the word of an oath	
	Sacrificed for themselves
Son forever	
	Weak

We have no better Priest than Yeshua. God wants us to know His Son, and the Son desires to draw us near to His Father. Don't delay. There is hope in the Son.

The diamond is the hardest gem, and it takes another diamond to break it. The hope we find in Yeshua is unbreakable. His hope is priceless. Most people would give everything they have for a little hope, yet Yeshua lavishes it on us. Just as light reflects off a diamond, causing it to glitter, we are to reflect the love and hope of Yeshua to the world.

Record anything the Lord spoke to or impressed upon you in this chapter.

_____

_____

_____

_____

Where is your hope placed? Is Yeshua your hope? If not, ask Him to be and believe with all your heart He lives for you.

Chapter 8 – Pearl
Purity, righteousness, holiness, and *the Bride of Christ*

Day One

One of the most famous pearls is the La Peregrina Pearl. For centuries, kings and queens owned and wore this tear-drop-shaped jewel. An African slave on the coast of the Isle of Santa Margarita in the Gulf of Panama found it in the sixteenth century and traded it for his freedom. The administrator of the Spanish colony gave it to Phillip II of Spain, who gave it to his wife, Mary I of England, as a wedding gift. After her death, the Crown of Spain owned the pearl for 250 years. Later Joseph Bonaparte, the king of Spain and Napoleon's brother, fled to Great Britain with the gem and other jewels when Spain defeated the French in the Battle of Vitoria. After 100 years in England, actor Richard Burton bought the pearl in 1969 and gave it to his wife, Elizabeth Taylor, for Valentine's Day. She had the La Peregrina Pearl set in a necklace with diamonds, rubies, and other pearls. Her gorgeous pendant sold for $11 million after her death.[1]

When an irritation such as a grain of sand enters the soft body of a mollusk, it covers the annoyance with a mother-of-pearl substance, called nacre, until a pearl forms.[2] This gem is a white, iridescent stone which means "purity, righteousness, holiness, and the Bride of Christ."[3]

Hebrews 8 is short, but it packs a punch. In this chapter, we will examine the Messianic Covenant and the tabernacle, and how these are significant to us now. We will read Exodus and Jeremiah to gather more priceless treasure about our Messiah. They promise rich meaning and invaluable understanding of Yeshua and His Word.

I cannot wait to share the meaning of the Tabernacle with you and to travel back in time together to see how its layout points us to the Son.

When I went to Israel, our group toured the Israel Museum and saw the model of the ancient city of Jerusalem. It was fascinating to imagine people walking around the temple, shopping in the markets, and gathering to listen to Yeshua at the Mount of Olives. Our tour guide took us to what would have been the southeast corner, or the pinnacle of the Temple. This was the place where Satan took Yeshua to tempt Him to throw Himself down (Luke 4:9). In its day, this place overlooked the Kidron Valley, or Valley of Judgement. On Yom Kippur, a priest pushed the scapegoat (yes, pushed) over the pinnacle into the Valley of Judgement. Ironically, Satan intended Yeshua to be the scapegoat instead of the Lamb.

The Tabernacle

Chapter 8 begins by reiterating, *We have such a high priest...* from Hebrews 7:26. Yeshua is holy (pure), innocent (without fault or blameless), unstained (undefiled or pure), separated from sinners (departed, removed), and exalted above the Heavens (high, lofty).[4]

Please read **Hebrews 8:1-2.**

How did the author refer to God in verse 1?

_____

How is our High Priest described in these two verses?

_____
_____
_____

The word *minister* in the Greek language means, a "servant, a minister, or one who cares for another, implying special duties."[5] Look at **Hebrews 8:2**.

Where does Yeshua act as a minister or servant?

_____

How does the author describe the true Tent or Tabernacle in this verse?

_____

Yeshua is a minister in the Holy Place within the Tabernacle of God. This is not the earthly tabernacle. The word *tabernacle* means *to dwell*. John used it in **John 1:14**: *The Word became flesh and dwelt (tabernacled) among us.* One other point I want to make before moving on is in **John 1:11**. Please read this verse.

Who did not receive Yeshua?

_____

In his book, *The Jewish Gospel of John*, Eli Lizorkin-Eyzenberg explains the Greek word for "his own people" is better translated to mean Yeshua's tribe, or the Judeans.[6] It was the tribe of Judah who did not receive Him. Overall, many Israelites accepted Yeshua. He came first for the Jews. In Matthew 15:24, Yeshua told the Canaanite woman, *I was sent only to the lost sheep of the house of Israel.* He came for Israel, and He sent Israel to the Gentile world (Matt. 28:19-20).

Yeshua may have come first for the Jews, but He came for the entire world. The Jewish people were the first evangelists. Just think what would have happened had they not shared the good news of the Messiah with the world.

Pearl - Day Two
Purity, righteousness, holiness, and *the Bride of Christ*

In Joshua 13-21, God had Joshua place the twelve Tribes throughout Israel. Judah was south of Jerusalem, between the Dead and Mediterranean Seas. If you lived at the time of Yeshua, you entered the Temple from the land of Judah.

As you crossed the threshold, you came to the square, bronze altar where the priest waited to offer your lamb as a sacrifice. He laid it on the altar, and you "crushed" its head with your hands to transfer your sin to the perfect, white lamb (refer to Chapter 6, Day One). We can now see this altar as our sacrifice of praise, or where we surrender our hopes, dreams, future, spouse, children, or job to God in prayer.

Next, you came to the bronze basin for washing. Before entering the Holy Place, you washed your hands and feet; you must be clean. Exodus 30:21 says, *They shall wash their hands and their feet, so they may not die. It shall be a statute forever to them, even to him [Aaron] and his offspring throughout their generations.* Yeshua washed us clean once and for all as our Lamb. As we enter this place in our imperfection, we wash by confessing and repenting for our sin each day as we spend time with the Father. Now we are clean to enter the Holy Place.

As you walked through the veil into the Holy Place, you saw the menorah on your left, with its seven lamps lighting your way to the Holy of Holies. We will never again walk in darkness because Yeshua is the Light of the World (John 8:12). On your right, the gold table held the steaming bread of the Presence. The warm, moist air from the fresh, baked artisan bread surrounded you. It's the true Bread from Heaven; the Bread of Life. You will never hunger once you have eaten this Bread (John 7:32-35).

Ahead was the altar of incense before the veil which led to the Holy of Holies. This golden table held a fragrance of sweet and spicy licorice. We are a sweet aroma to the Lord as Yeshua leads us into God's presence.

A thick veil made of blue, purple, and scarlet yarn with cherubim woven into it separated all but the high priest from the Most Holy Place. YHWH (YaHWeH) descended onto the gold-plated Ark of the Covenant and mercy seat. Never to be closed again, God ripped this veil from top to bottom, so we have access to Him (Luke 23:45). Our High Priest allows us to approach His throne with boldness to find grace and receive mercy in our time of need (Heb. 4:16).

When we pray, we approach God, starting from the outside courts and making our way to the innermost Holy of Holies. When God deals with us, He starts in our Holy of Holies out to our courts. When God addresses our needs, desires, or problems, He goes straight to our Holy of Holies (our heart and spirit) then out to our courts (physical body). But we approach God starting from the outside (praise and worship) to His intimate presence (His desires and will for us).

In prayer, I take my time getting to the heart of God. I worship the Father, Son, and Holy Spirit by reciting scriptural descriptions of them: *You are a good Father, worthy of praise, faithful and true, rich in mercy, loving, kind, compassionate, my Savior, Redeemer, Teacher, Helper...* I praise Him, reminding and thanking Him for answering prayers. Next, I confess and repent for my sins, as Yeshua washes off the grime of my sin so I can move toward intimacy with Him. As I step closer into His presence, I lift loved ones, my needs, my questions, my desires. I ask for truth, discernment, wisdom, and peace to know His will. I seek His heart for me and for those I love.

When God responds He goes right to my spirit. He takes care of my heart problems first. Sometimes, He reveals a motive behind my questions or hurt. The Lord may bring Scripture to my mind to answer my need or fill me with His love. He fills me with peace, calming my fears or distresses. God cares for my physical needs (or my court).

Write any ways you may add to or change how you approach God in prayer. Ask Him to inspire you to come to Him daily. Renew your commitment to seek Him.

_____

_____

_____

_____

_____

Gifts and Sacrifices

Let's read **Hebrews 8:3-4**. If you have ever read through Leviticus, you know the many offerings and sacrifices given by the priests. Glance at the chapter titles of the first six chapters and you will see grain, sin, and guilt offerings, among others, not to mention the various offerings for feasts in later chapters. All priests made offerings and sacrifices.

What did our priest, Yeshua, offer?

_____

Let's see what you remember from the previous two chapters of Hebrews. Why couldn't Yeshua be a priest when He was here on earth?

_____

Pearl - Day Three
Purity, righteousness, holiness, and *the Bride of Christ*

We see the word *shadow* used differently in Scripture. It can represent *our lives* as in Psalm 144:4 and Job 8:9; it also symbolizes *our protection* as in Psalm 91:1 and 57:1. But shadow can mean *death or the grave,* too as in Psalm 23 and Job 10:21-22. **Colossians 2:17** says, … *things which are a mere shadow of what is to come; but the substance belongs to Christ.* Both Colossians and Hebrews use the Greek word *skia* for *shadow* in this verse which means, "an image cast by an object and representing the form of that object."[7]

Hebrews 8:5 says, *They serve a copy [type] and shadow [skia] of the heavenly things.* As we have studied, the priests who served at the Tent of Meeting or Temple were types and shadows of Yeshua.

What else in **Hebrews 8:5** is a type and shadow of heavenly things?

_____

Where did Moses see it before?

_____

Please turn to **Exodus 24:15-18.** Where is Moses?

_____

Now, please read **Exodus 25:1-9.** What did God show Moses?

_____

The Hebrew word for *pattern* is *tav'niyt* and translates as "pattern, form, likeness, or figure."[8] Its root word, *banah,* means "begin to build (-er), obtain children, and make."[9] Why does this word refer to children? How does this fit with the *pattern* God gave Moses? Many believe, me included, that God showed Moses the real Tabernacle on the mountain. The real Tabernacle is Yeshua. Remember, tabernacle is *to dwell.* In the Old Testament, God dwelt with His people in the Tent of Meeting. In the New Testament, Yeshua dwelt with His people in the flesh. The tabernacle was a shadow of the Messiah.

In **John 2:19,** how does Yeshua refer to Himself?

_____

Since the time of Yeshua's ascension, we are the temple of the Holy Spirit. He dwells within us.

There is one more thing I want to explain about the tabernacle from C.J. Lovik, author of *The Living Word in 3D.*[10] (Paraphrased)

The Hebrew word for tabernacle is *mischan,* spelled משבן. Reading right to left, the letters are mem, shin, kaf, and nun. Just as we saw in Chapter 1 with the word Elohim, mischan's letters represent meaningful pictures. The first letter *mem,* מ (pronounced mim) is defined as "comes down from Heaven," like water or rain. As we saw in Chapter 3, when *mem* joins with the *nun,* נ (pronounced noon) meaning "life," it spells *manna,* מן. Second is ש or *shin.* Characterized by teeth, it signifies destruction. *Shin* (pronounced sheen) is spelled שׁ and represents the destruction of life or a *sacrifice.* Next is *kaf* (pronounced with a guttural k) and its picture describes a hand over the mouth as in refusing to pass judgment. The word *kaf* is spelled כף and symbolizes *atonement.* The last letter *nun* is spelled וין and depicts, "Life that gives life."

Within the word for Tabernacle, we have:
Manna: Comes down from Heaven to give life.

Mem: Comes down from Heaven
Shin: Destruction of life or Sacrifice.
Kaf: Atonement.
Nun: Life that gives life.

This is Yeshua!

The New Covenant

Here is **Hebrews 8:6** in the New Living Translation: *But God gave our High Priest a ministry that is far superior to the ministry of those who serve under the old laws, for he is the one who guarantees for us a better covenant with God, based on better promises.*
You can read it in your Bible, too. Look at what the writer refers to as *superior* or *better* regarding Yeshua.

What are the three better and/or superior things mentioned in this verse?
_____
_____

As mentioned before, Yeshua is a better priest than those of the tabernacle and temple. Now, let's look at the old covenant found in the Law. The Mosaic covenant was between God and Israel, which Moses mediated for them.

Read **Exodus 24:3-8** and **Leviticus 17:10-11**.

Exodus 24:6 refers to the Law as the Book of the Covenant. How do the people respond to what Moses reads? _____

In **Exodus 24:7-8**, what does Moses call the blood he throws on them? Why is this important?
_____
_____

In **Leviticus 17:10-11**, what does the blood do for the people? How does it do it?
_____
_____

Moses read the Word of God to them, and, by their agreement, the people made a covenant with God. The blood linked them together just as Yeshua's blood links us with Him in the Messianic covenant, the better covenant.

Pearl - Day Four
Purity, righteousness, holiness, and *the Bride of Christ*

After a hard work week, what do you look forward to? For some of you it may be rest, or sleeping in on Saturday, for others it may be running around and having fun. We read in Hebrews 4 about the promised rest for the Israelites. If you recall, Canaan was God's Promised Land where the remaining Israelites would live after the captivity of Egypt and wandering the wilderness for forty years.

What is the promise Yeshua gave to His followers in **John 14:3-4**?

_____

Which is the better promise? _____

We have a superior Priest, a superior covenant, and a superior promise of rest and a place to live for eternity. This is what Hebrews 8:6 is talking about. Where would we be without Yeshua?

Hebrews 8:7 says, *For if that first covenant had been faultless, then there would have been no occasion to look for a second.*

Turn to **Romans 8:2-3**, please. According to this verse, what was the Law's limitation?

_____

Romans 8:4 explains Yeshua fulfilled the righteous requirement of the Law in us. His blood could do what the blood of animals could not. The Law showed us it was impossible to be holy, but through Yeshua, we can be. There are those who say Yeshua did away with the whole Law. Although there is no longer any reason to sacrifice a lamb or goat, the rituals, ceremonies, feasts, and Temple still have a place in the life of a Messianic Jew when those things are in existence.

Let's look at verses concerning the New Covenant. Turn to and read **Mark 14:22-24** and **Luke 22:19-20**. This is the Messianic covenant. We remember this covenant every time we take communion. It is a part of the Passover meal (Pesach, in Hebrew). If you haven't done it, I encourage you to go to a Jewish Seder meal. It is an enlightening experience.

In my mid-twenties, I went to a Seder for the first time. Our church arranged for a Messianic rabbi to come to our church and have the Pesach with our young adult group. The rabbi gave us booklets to follow along in English as he read in Hebrew. Most of the meal recounts the story of the Exodus. However, there are just as many things that point to Messiah.

There were five symbolic foods on the seder plate. A *lamb shank* reminds us of the blood the Hebrew slaves put on the door frames to protect themselves from the angel of death. Yeshua was the Lamb slain to save us.

We ate a significant amount of the *bitter herbs,* which are so strong it will make you cry, to recall the bitterness of slavery. But we are no longer slaves to sin because Yeshua is our Savior.

There were three pieces of *unleavened bread* or *matzah* representing the Father, Son, and Holy Spirit, to us. The host took the middle matzah, cracked it in half and wrapped one half in linen, then hid it for the children to find later. This embodied Yeshua, broken, wrapped in linen, put in a tomb, and resurrecting after three days. The host or father gave a reward to the child who discovered the broken matzah. He broke it into small pieces and shared it among those at the table. In Luke 22:19, Yeshua said, *"This is my body broken for you"* as He passed these pieces out among His disciples.

Parsley dipped in salt water conveys the Children of Israel's life of tears. After the Jews returned from Babylon, they added a *hard-boiled egg* to the Seder. It signified the fertility god of the Babylonians.

(Could this be why we include eggs in Easter?) After the bitter herbs and salty parsley the *charoset* was a welcome sweet taste to your mouth. It comprised of a mixture of apples, nuts, honey, and cinnamon, and it symbolized the mortar used between the bricks the Hebrews made for the Egyptians.

There are four cups of wine or grape juice. We drank the first cup with the blessing (Luke 22:17-18).

The second cup helped us remember the ten plagues. We put one drop of juice on our napkins with our pinkies as we repeated each plague. There was a feast between the second and third cups. We had a potluck the first time, but other times I have done this we had a traditional Jewish meal and ate way too much good food! A Jewish family has the same traditional banquet each year.

The third cup is the Cup of Redemption, and we drank it after supper. It represented the cup Yeshua used to symbolize the New Covenant in Luke 22:20. They would have eaten the pieces of the hidden matzah before this cup, which resembles our communion.

Last, the fourth cup is the Cup of Hallel or praise.[11] Pesach is both a solemn and celebratory event remembered every year by the Jewish family. God commanded His people to do this forever (Ex. 12:14).

Pearl - Day Five
Purity, righteousness, holiness, and *the Bride of Christ*

The prophet Jeremiah warned the king and people of Judah of the coming destruction and exile at the hands of the Babylonian king, Nebuchadnezzar. Does it surprise you no one believed him? The Israelite people rejected, persecuted, threw Jeremiah in a cistern, and later forced him to leave Jerusalem.

Jeremiah wrote the words of God to His people in Jeremiah 29:11, *For I know the plans I have for you, declares the Lord, plans for welfare and not for evil, to give you a future and a hope.* Can you imagine reading these words after an evil king steals, kills, and destroys everything you know and love and sends you to another country to be a slave?

God wanted to assure them He continued to be with them even though they were in exile. In Jeremiah 31, God promised to gather them back into their country and be their God. He pledged to bring them together under a new covenant — a better covenant.

The Shema

In **Hebrews 8:8**, the author says, *For he finds fault with them... He* is God. Who is *them*?

_____

Hebrews 8:8-12 is a quote from **Jeremiah 31:31-34**. There are minor differences between the original Hebrew and the translation into Greek then English. I encourage you to read it in the Old Testament.

Read **Hebrews 8:8-12**. With whom is God making this new covenant?

_____

Verse 9 tells us this covenant will not be like the old Mosaic covenant. Why?

_____

Let's compare **Hebrews 8:10-12** with **Deuteronomy 6:4-15**. In verses 4 and 5 of Deuteronomy 6 is the *Shema*. It is the first word of Deuteronomy 6:4, Hear, *O Israel*. In this verse, God commands Israel to listen and obey or to keep His covenant. When the people of God say shema, we mean, "I will listen and do what you say," or "I will keep your covenant."[12]

In **Deuteronomy 6:6-9**, what does God command of His people concerning His Word?

_____

_____

_____

In **Hebrews 8:10**, what will God do?

_____

_____

Contrast **Hebrews 8:11** and **Deuteronomy 6:7**. What was changed in the commands?

_____

_____

Last, look at the difference between **Hebrews 8:12** and **Deuteronomy 6:15**.

What does the new covenant include that was not there in the old? (The answer is not found written in these verses.) _____

This covenant was first for the Jew, then the Gentile. If you are a believer and follower of Yeshua, you are part of the Church; you are His Bride. God will put His law into our minds and write them on our hearts through His Word and Holy Spirit. He is our God and we are His people. We will all know Him, from the least of us to the greatest. He will be merciful toward our sin and will choose not to remember it when we repent of it.

Our salvation is not a onetime prayer. It is a life of *faithfulness* and *shema*. It is abiding in Yeshua as He abides in us. He loves you more than His own life.

The Pearl of Great Price

Hebrews 8:13, says, *In speaking of a new covenant, he makes the first one obsolete.*
Who makes the first one obsolete? _____

Who or what makes the old covenant obsolete?

_____

In the second part of verse 13, the word for *vanish away* means *to cease to exist*.[13] The author wrote the Book of Hebrews before the destruction of the temple. Yeshua prophesied there would be no stone on top another (Matt. 24:2). We know the Romans demolished it, and there has not been another temple or sacrifice made since that time.

The new covenant includes grace and the Holy Spirit. Without them, we would be no better than the people of the Old Testament, or old covenant. As Paul says in **2 Corinthians 5:17**, *Therefore, if anyone is in Christ, he is a new creation. The old has passed away; behold, the new has come.* This is God's way.

In **Matthew 13:52**, Yeshua says, *Therefore every scribe who has been trained for the Kingdom of Heaven is like a master of a house who brings out of his treasure what is new and what is old.* (Emphasis mine)

Did you see the word *trained* in that verse? Studying the Word as we wait upon the Holy Spirit to teach us is one way He trains us. Trials, suffering, and relationships train us. We are to be scribes and teachers of the Word by using the things God taught and instilled in us through our challenges and tribulations.

Of the jewels we have read about up until now, some have been thousands of years old and others more recent. Both are valuable, but sometimes the value increased because of its history or by adding other stones. This is the Kingdom of Heaven. It is already priceless because of the Father, Son, and Holy Spirit. As we learn and understand God's "history" and that of His people, it adds worth and richness to our hearts. God is about the new *and* the old. He forgets nothing, yet chooses not to remember our past.

The Kingdom of Heaven is like a merchant in search of fine pearls, who, on finding one pearl of great value, sold all he had and bought it. (Matt. 13:45-46). Have you found the pearl of great value?

Yeshua is that pearl.

How does the pearl relate to this chapter?

_____

_____

_____

Chapter 9- Ruby
Blood, salvation, redemption, and *sacrifice*

Day One

The Carmen Lúcia Ruby is an exquisite jewel with a deep red color called "pigeon's blood" set in a platinum ring. Weighing in at 23.10 carats, it features two triangular diamonds at over one carat each mounted on either side of an oval ruby. Carmen Lúcia Buck was a collector of jewels. While undergoing cancer treatment in 2002, she decided she would buy the ruby ring to celebrate her recovery. But that never happened because she died in 2003. Her husband, Dr. Peter Buck, founder of the Subway restaurant chain, bought the stunning jewelry and donated it to the Smithsonian in his beloved wife's honor.[1]

Large rubies of twenty carats or more are rare. The ruby's color affects its value. It is said the color must resemble blood, specifically the first two drops of blood from a freshly killed pigeon.[2]

A pigeon was the Temple sacrifice for the poor in the days of the Bible. Most of this chapter will be about the blood and sacrifice of goats and bulls. The ruby's color symbolizes *blood, salvation, redemption, and sacrifice.*[3]

The blood of goats, lambs, and bulls is not a part of our lives unless you raise livestock for a living or are a farm veterinarian. Most of us never deal with the blood of animals.

My husband and I raise dairy goats. Our numbers have shrunk due to our "help" going off to college. We went from a herd of fourteen to three goats. My daughter loves the goats but is not around much anymore to help. I take care of the day-to-day feeding and milking. Although he helps me, my husband gets stuck with the dirty job of cleaning out the barn. When I read passages in the Bible about goats and/or sheep, I have a good understanding of the analogies.

One myth people believe is goats eat anything. However, goats are finicky. They may *taste* everything, but they do not eat everything. Goats are like dogs, as they learn their names and will come to you when called. Some are vocal and will let you know when something is not "right." We had a young goat get out of the pasture one day and our goat Jeri let us know about it. She came to the fence and yelled at me every time she saw me, until I walked over to her and saw a little one was out.

As hard as I try to keep them healthy, they are prone to parasites and diseases. Goat vets are not available in our area since we live in a residential neighborhood. As a result, I have become our "goat doc." I have done a lot of research and am part of Facebook's goat groups to learn what I need. I give shots, help my husband disbud (which is burning off the horn cells from a kid's head), and have had to even "go in" to turn a breach baby. This life is not for the faint of heart.

We will discuss more about these animals in this chapter, so we will return to this story. In Hebrews 9, we will look once again at the new covenant and the two "tents." We will take an in-depth view into the Holy of Holies, the Ark of the Covenant, and the blood of Christ.

The Most Holy Place

Let's start by reading **Hebrews 9:1**. The word *regulations* in the first verse can also mean requirements or commandments. In recent chapters, we read under the first covenant God had requirements for offerings, sacrifices, and tithing. All these fall under worship. It is easy to think worship is singing along to great praise music on Sunday morning. But it is more than that. The definition of worship according to Google is, "the feeling or expression of reverence and adoration for a deity."[4] Singing, tithing, offerings, and even the sacrifice of our time, money, or gifts for God are all part of the way we worship our Creator.

In John 4, Yeshua talks with the Samaritan woman at the well. He explains worship under the Messianic covenant in **John 4:23-24**.

How will true worshippers worship the Father?

_____

Why? _____

In light of these verses, what does worship mean to you?

_____
_____
_____

We worship in spirit by the Holy Spirit. God is spirit, so we use the Spirit within us to worship Him. This means using the gifts of the Spirit (1 Cor. 12 & 14), as well as our God-given gifts and talents, such as singing, playing instruments, service, and giving generously, among others.

Look at a few verses on truth and give the main idea of the verse below.

Isaiah 65:16 _____

John 14:6 _____

John 16:13 _____

2 Timothy 2:15 _____

Ruby - Day Two
Blood, salvation, redemption, and sacrifice

In the second part of **Hebrews 9:1** through **9:2**, holiness was an earthly place found in the tabernacle.

What is the first section called, and how is it described?

_____

_____

Turn to **Exodus 25:23-30**. What is this table made of? _____

Brad Scott, of Wildbranch Ministry, explains the acacia wood this way:

> The ark is to be made of '*tzey shittiym* or shittim wood. This word is sometimes translated as acacia wood, which may or may not be the same wood that Yeshua's wreath of thorns was constructed from. It also was the thorny branches placed over the sheep pens at night and during the winter months that Yeshua referred to in Yochanan [John] 10:8-17. This tree grows very deep roots, draws nourishment from deep in the earth, and survives very well in dry ground. This tree is not an attractive tree such as a mighty oak or a giant redwood. In the Septuagint translation (Greek Old Testament) of the Scriptures, shittim is translated as *aphthartos* or incorruptible.
>
> This shittim wood speaks of the Messiah's perfect humanity. This wood was touched with all that nature could throw against it, as it was, and is, with all trees, yet remained undefiled and incorruptible.[5]

What Brad Scott is saying is the acacia wood used to make the Ark for the Temple was a hard wood with deep roots and thorny branches. These thorny branches were used as a wall for the cave or pen the sheep were in at night to protect them from predators. Acacia's unsightly hard wood protected the tree from parasites and whatever nature threw at it, while it remained unaffected. Its deep roots helped it survive the arid climate.

Brad gives two passages to go with this teaching. In these two verses, you will see how we can compare Yeshua to the nature of the acacia tree. Please read them and record how they coincide with his teaching on the acacia wood.

Isaiah 53:2

_____

_____

Hebrews 7:26

_____

_____

I hope you can see why God had them use a tree that resembled the character and "appearance" of His Son—undefiled, incorruptible, strong, protector, and deep-rooted.

They used this same wood to make the bronze altar and the Altar of Incense, as well as all poles and pillars. These things were covered with gold or bronze.

If you were to read about each of these items in Exodus, you would find each was made with four rings and two poles. Why do you think that is?

_____

The first curtain led into the Holy Place. Everything in there was holy, and the priest entered this place daily. Let's read **Hebrews 9:3-5**.

In verse 4, it appears the author placed the Altar of Incense in the Most Holy Place. But, examining the Greek meaning of the word *having* or *had* beginning the verse, it means *neighboring*. The Altar of Incense neighbors the second curtain going into the Holy of Holies. It is in the Holy Place, as mentioned in the last chapter.

What is in the Holy of Holies?

_____

What three items were in the Ark?

_____
_____

A Sign for the Rebels

We will turn to **Numbers 17** and read the first eleven verses. First, let's look at **Numbers 16**. A group of 250 men led by Korah, (a Levite), Dathan, Abriam, and On, from the tribe of Reuben, revolted against Moses. They were angry because not all Levites were priests. Korah thought they were holy enough to be in the priesthood, as well, and felt Moses and Aaron exalted themselves above them. Moses was angry. He asked Korah why being set apart by God as Levites was not enough for him. Why did he demand they be priests, too? Moses told him their problem was not with him, but with God. God told Moses and Aaron to step away and have everyone else who was near these men back away. God opened a hole in the earth to swallow Korah, Dathan, Abriam, On, and their wives and children. Fire consumed the 250 men who conspired with them, too.

You would think it was the end of that, but no. The next day the rest of the people of Israel were mad with Moses and Aaron because *they* killed "the people of the LORD." This time God sent a plague which killed 14,700 people before Aaron made atonement for them and stopped the curse.

How often are we similar? We blame those in authority when we do not get what we want because God keeps it from happening. We can be disappointed with what appears to be lack of favor He has shown us and want more.

Years ago, after starting in a new church, I looked forward to teaching Bible studies. It seemed every time I wanted to have a class on a particular theme or book of the Bible, our pastor let us know he would preach or hold a class on it. It seemed to be the same thing I wanted to do. A few times, I told him my idea or emailed him information for his permission beforehand. I got so mad. I knew he had it in for me. He refused to let me use my gift! This went on for a while. I could not believe it.

One Sunday morning, finding it hard to worship, I grumbled to God concerning this man. Suddenly, in my spirit I heard God say, "He (my pastor) didn't say 'no,' I DID!" *Oh. Okay. I'm sorry*— was all I could muster. God made it clear; it was His doing, not my pastor's doing. I had to change my attitude. I no longer blamed him, but saw it was God's timing and will I had to align with.

Have you ever been in a similar situation? Has God ever kept you from something and you blamed it on someone else? Or has God said "no" to you, only to realize later He protected you?

_____
_____

Ruby - Day Three
Blood, salvation, redemption, and sacrifice

Growing up, I was small for my age and was often asked how old I was. Even in college, while home on break, someone asked me why I wasn't in high school that day. In elementary school, I dreaded when it came time for team sports at recess. As the teacher-chosen "captain" started picking their team members one-by-one, I knew I would be somewhere at the end. It was a good day if I was second to last instead of last. Sometimes it can still feel as though God uses the same method of choosing His "team." But Scripture tells us God uses the weak to shame the strong (1 Cor. 1:27). He does things the opposite way of man.

Today, we will continue our lesson by reading **Numbers 17**. God ends the grumbling against Moses and Aaron once for all.

How did God show the people who He chose?

_____

_____

What instructions did God give Moses concerning Aaron's staff?

_____

What was this a sign for?

_____

Lastly, let's read **Numbers 18:1-5**.

In verse 1, how does God explain the priest's duty concerning the sanctuary and priesthood?

_____

_____

This verse is foreshadowing the Messiah. In verse 2, the tribe of Levi aided the priests with their duties in the tabernacle, as we partner with Yeshua as fellow priests of His Kingdom.

In **Numbers 18:3-5**, the sanctuary as well as its vessels are holy.

What happens if Levites other than priests touch the vessels of the tabernacle?

_____

God gave the priesthood and Levites to Aaron and his sons as a gift (Num. 18: 6-7). As it was their duty to guard over the sanctuary and its receptacles, they suffered the punishment (iniquities) when failing those responsibilities. No one could touch the holy vessels or anything within the veil and live. The people of Israel approached God through the priests in the Holy Place and the high priest in the Holy of Holies. No one went in on their own or God would kill them.

The Cherubim

Please go back to **Hebrews 9:5**. Remember we are discussing the Ark of the Covenant from verse 4.

What is above it?

Please turn to and read **Exodus 25:17-22**. Try to picture how this looked. Imagine a cherub at each end of the cover, spreading their wings like a canopy over the Mercy Seat, covering something placed or sitting between them.

Please go back to **Hebrews 9:6-7**. The first and second sections referred to in these verses are the Holy Place and Holy of Holies.

In the Holy of Holies, where does the high priest offer the sacrifice?

_____

Turn to **John 20:11-12**.

Where is Mary? _____

Whom does she see? Where are they?

_____

Do you see the similarities between the Mercy Seat and the place inside the tomb?

How does this affect the way you see God?

_____

_____

God knew what He was doing when He had Moses build the Ark and Mercy Seat. He knew the place His Son's body would lay from the beginning of time.

I heard this teaching a while ago, and it floored me. It cemented in me an awe of God's ways.

Let's read **Hebrews 9:6-10**. I find it helps to read Scripture in more than one version of the Bible. Here are those verses in the New Living Translation (NLT):

> 6. When these things were all in place, the priests went in and out of the first room regularly as they performed their religious duties. 7. But only the high priest goes into the Most Holy Place, and only once a year, and always with blood, which he offers to God to cover his own sins and the sins the people have committed in ignorance. 8. By these regulations, the Holy Spirit revealed that the Most Holy Place was not open to the people as long as the first room and the entire system it represents were still in use. 9. This is an illustration pointing to the present time. For the gifts and sacrifices that the priests offer are not able to cleanse the consciences of the people who bring them. 10. For that old system deals only with food and drink and ritual washing—external regulations that are in effect only until their limitations can be corrected.

In verse 6, the religious duties of the priests were to light the oil of the lampstand, replace the showbread with fresh bread of the Sabbath, and burn incense on the altar in the morning and evening. Verse 7 refers to Yom Kippur, which we have discussed in other chapters.

In verse 8, the verb *indicates* or *revealed* is present tense, which means the Holy Spirit *continually indicates* or *reveals*. The phrase, *as long as the first room and the entire system it represents were still in use* means, "as long as approach depends on Levitical-ceremonies."[6] When the people of Israel approached God through the priests, the Most Holy Place was not open to them. When we try to come near God through *works* instead of Yeshua, He is not accessible. Verse 9 says this illustration points to now, our time.

What was wrong with the gifts and sacrifices the priests offered?

_____

_____

In verse 10, how were the external regulations corrected?

_____

_____

The Greater and more Perfect Tent

We need to talk about blood. The spilling of an animal's blood is in no way an ordinary thing for most of us. To euthanize a pet, a vet uses an injection to put them "to sleep." It is common for a farmer or rancher to shoot sick, injured, or dying cattle to put them out of their misery. However, that is not the way they performed sacrifices in biblical times. It was messy.

Goats, sheep, and cattle do not die quietly when sacrificed by the priests. Even though these animals are livestock, it is possible to get attached to them. Imagine having to hold down your favorite, perfect lamb as the priest slit its throat. Its blood soaked you and the priest as it cried out in pain. Not a pleasant thought, I know. This was Israel's reality.

We can remove ourselves from the horrific death Yeshua went through, too. We weren't there to witness it, but His blood splashed on us. The nails held Him on the cross, then His side was slit, and blood and water poured out. He cried out, *"Father forgive them, for they know not what they do"* (Luke 23:34).

Few of us could watch an animal sacrifice, let alone a man tortured to death. But it was routine during the time of the Bible.

Have you ever considered how you might have responded if you were in Jerusalem at the time of Yeshua's crucifixion? Would you have screamed, "Crucify Him!" or begged for Him to be saved?

_____

_____

Ruby - Day Four
Blood, salvation, redemption, and *sacrifice*

With streaming services like Netflix and Hulu, we can watch TV programs from twenty or thirty years ago anytime we want. Shows like *Friends*, which my husband and I watched all the time during its first run in the nineties, are now being watched by a whole new generation. It's funny to see the actors using large mobile phones with long antennae, and the hair and clothing styles, too. It can really make you glad some things have changed.

If you compare TV shows from the seventies and eighties to shows from the nineties, like *Friends*, until present day, we see our culture becoming desensitized to topics like premarital sex and homosexuality. I wish the innocence of the older shows would have stayed the same.

Please read **Hebrews 9:11-15**. Today, we are going to see a series of contrasts of new and old. The old things were a shadow and type of what was to come, but the new has come and has done what the old could not.

According to **Hebrews 9:11,** what are the two "old" things improved upon?

In verse 12, what is contrasted? _____

What did Yeshua secure with His blood?

Verses 13 and 14 go together. What was purified with the blood of goats and bulls? What was purified with the blood of Christ?

The offering of goats and bulls refers to the offerings done on Yom Kippur. The phrase *ashes of a heifer* refer to a normal sin offering done on an occasional basis. Both types of sacrifices only purified the flesh. It could not go beyond the surface.

Yeshua's sacrifice went/goes further to cleanse the mind (conscience) and spirit.[7] His blood brings healing to every part of us. It removes the guilt and shame of our sin.

Through whom did Yeshua offer Himself to God (vs 14)?

In verse 15, what do those who are called receive?

Why do they receive it?

Do you notice the three "eternals"? They are eternal redemption, eternal Spirit, and eternal inheritance. Redemption means, "The action of saving or being saved from sin, error, or evil."[8] Yeshua's redemption is eternal; He continually saves, or heals and restores us from our flesh, sickness, spiritual death, and the evil in this world. His Spirit eternally teaches, comforts, helps, and intercedes for us.

Through Yeshua, we have an eternal inheritance in Heaven waiting for you and me.

If the Temple were still standing and the priests were offering daily sacrifices, nothing they did would have eternal value. It is only through Yeshua and His blood that there is eternal significance.

Blood of the Covenant

In **Hebrews 9:16-22**, we will study how blood was used in the Mosaic covenant. First, in verse 15, the author spoke of the eternal inheritance.

The Bible Exposition Commentary says:

"The word 'covenant' not only means 'an agreement,' but it also carries the idea of 'a last will and testament.' If a man writes his will, that will is not in force until he dies. It was necessary for Jesus Christ to die so the terms of the New Covenant might be enforced. 'This cup is the new testament [covenant, will] in my blood, which is shed for you' (Luke 22:20)."[9]

The covenant Yeshua made functions as a will. Where there's a will, there is an inheritance. In verses 16 and 17, he speaks of the conditions for a will to be executed. What are those conditions?

_____

Let's go back to the three "eternals" mentioned in **Hebrews 9:12, 14,** and **15**. When I see a word repeated like that, it tells me there is a point to be made in these verses. What's the opposite of eternal? *Temporary.* Under the first covenant, redemption was temporary; the work of the Spirit was temporary, and there was only a temporary inheritance based on their earthly life. Everything connected with the earthly tent was short-lived. Everything connected with the Heavenly Tent is eternal.

What does verse 18 tell us about the first covenant?

_____

_____

Verses 19-22 refer to **Exodus 24:3-8,** with some added information. We have read Exodus 23:20-22, already. In Exodus 23:23-33, God explained to Moses His intention to drive out the people of Canaan before the Children of Israel. He promised to bless them with children, good health, and land. He forbade Moses and the Israelites to make any *covenant* with the gods of the people He drove out, nor did He allow them to dwell among them. He wanted their obedience. *Why?* He was making a covenant with them. To be in covenant with more than one god was like being married to two people at once. God wanted their love and faithfulness to be for Him only.

Read **Exodus 24:1-8**, please.

What does Moses do with the blood from the oxen?

_____

What do the people say in response to the reading of the Book of the Covenant?

_____

The Hebrew word used here for *obedient* is shema, to hear. The Book of the Covenant refers to the Ten Commandments and the laws following it in Exodus 20-23:19. The people said, *We will do what we hear the Lord saying in His Law.*

Will you?

Ruby - Day Five
Blood, salvation, redemption, and *sacrifice*

In both **Hebrews 9:20** and **Exodus 24:8**, what does Moses call what the LORD made with His people? _____

Now turn to **Matthew 26:26-28**. What does Yeshua call the cup?

_____

In **Hebrews 9:22**, what was blood used for?

_____

Do you see how important it was to involve blood in purification and covenant between God and His people? A blood covenant was a bond between God and the people, whether it was in the days of Moses, the days of Yeshua, or now.

Blood is life. The blood of a perfect animal was important to God for purification of the vessels in the tabernacle. The blood of His perfect Son gives us life and is even more significant to God. It joins us to the Son and the Father, allows for our holiness, and the forgiveness of sin.

Next, read **Hebrews 9:23**. This verse will set the stage for the rest of the verses in the paragraph. The "copies" are the vessels in the tabernacle that represent heavenly things. The blood of oxen purified them.

What is the better sacrifice? _____

The word sacrifice is plural in Hebrews 9:23. Even though there was only one sacrifice by Yeshua, it was multi-layered and widespread in its application and effect. [10]

The author of Hebrews implies Yeshua's blood purified the heavenly things. To help you appreciate this, you must understand the blood purified nothing during the time of Moses or the Temple periods. *The blood changed God's relationship to it.*[11]

Yeshua's blood does the same for us. We are still sinners like the rest of the world but allowing Yeshua's blood to cover our sin changes God's relationship with us. He no longer sees us as unclean; He sees the blood. We have the same hurts, fears, and pain as the rest of the world, but Yeshua's blood allows God to heal and restore us. The Holy Spirit has always existed, but once Yeshua ascended to Heaven, the blood allowed His presence to fill our hearts and lives.

Let's move on to **Hebrews 9:24-26**.

In these verses, with whom is Christ compared?

_____

Do you see how Yeshua was able "to put away sin" once for all? His blood covers our sin and changes how God sees us. Because of this, we "appear" clean to God, who sees Yeshua's blood instead of our sin. This is why we can approach Him and His throne to be in His presence. Yeshua is the priest who entered *the* Holy Place and sacrificed Himself.

Does this change how you approach God? Why?

_____

Turn to **Revelation 5:1-12**. Please hear these words with your heart. Do you hear the emotion?

Who are they worshipping? How is He portrayed?

_____

Record who is in this scene.

_____
_____

In **Revelation 1:13-16,** describes Yeshua differently. Why didn't they worship Yeshua in this form instead of a blood-covered, slain Lamb? His blood had the most power in the entire universe. No one could do what Yeshua and His blood did for humanity. That is why John weeps in Revelation 5. He sees no one worthy to open the scroll. NO ONE at all.

Revelation 5:5 says, *Weep no more; behold, the Lion of the tribe of Judah, the Root of David, has conquered, so he can open the scroll and its seven seals.*

What has He conquered?

_____

I should have given you many more lines for that last question, right? There are multiple answers. Yeshua has conquered all death and evil. We may die physically, but death is not the end!

Read the last two verses of **Hebrews 9**. Verse 27 gets used out of the context of this chapter, at times. I've heard it used to explain who the *two witnesses* from Revelation 11 will be. There have been a couple of Old Testament men who did not die. God supernaturally took them to Heaven. But I think this verse speaks to Yeshua's humanity.

He is God, but He was man. That is why the title *Son of Man* is fitting for Him. He was like man, but more. It was a Messianic title the people of His culture and time would have understood. It describes a redeemer, man, and King.[12]

According to verse 28, why is Yeshua appearing a second time?

_____

Look at **Hebrews 9:24, 26,** and **28**. What word do you see repeated?

_____

Do you see these words are used in the present, past, and future tenses? Time has no effect on the Godhead. Yeshua is working out our past; He is standing on our behalf now and will come to take us in our future. Our salvation is a continuous thing. We were saved when He shed His blood, died, and was resurrected, we are being saved as He stands on our behalf before God, and will save us when He returns and takes home we who are waiting for Him.

We read a lot about blood in this chapter. There is no one verse to represent the ruby. This chapter was all about sacrifice, redemption, blood, and salvation. I hope seeing a ruby or any other red stone will remind you of the sacrifice, blood, redemption, and salvation Yeshua offered for and to you. If there was a verse or "ruby" that spoke to you in this chapter, write it down to share.

_____
_____
_____

Colossians 2:3: *In whom (Yeshua) are hidden all the treasures of wisdom and knowledge*

Chapter 10 - Golden Diamond
The divine nature of Yeshua, glory and faith of the saints

Day One

Gold. Who doesn't love the shine and brilliance of it? Imagine it in a diamond. The *Incomparable* diamond necklace is a stunning piece of jewelry with ninety-one white diamonds weighing over 200 carats and designed to look like a vine with the almost 408-carat golden diamond hanging from it.[1]

Its owners gave this necklace's centerpiece, egg-sized gem the name *Incomparable* because it is internally flawless and the third largest diamond in the world.[2] It was found in a rubbish pile by a poor Congolese girl as a nearly 900-carat stone.[3]

The word incomparable means *beyond comparison; matchless* or *unequaled*.[4] Like this jewel, Yeshua is unequaled in all He did and still does. The beautiful golden hue symbolizes the *divine nature of Yeshua, glory* and *faith of the saints*. [5]

When I was in high school and the teacher left the overhead projector on (you may or may not know what that is), students liked to put their hands in front of the light as shapes appeared on the screen as the shadow of a rabbit, a dog, or a bird. Here, the true form was the hands, not an animal. If I stood in front of a light, you would see my shadow, a black outline of my body with no definition or color. It is not me. I have blue eyes, light skin and hair, and love to wear blue jeans.

This is similar to the Law or the first covenant. It was a shadow of the real thing, the real "thing" being the Son of God and His covenant. Because it was a shadow did not diminish its importance or give us the right to dismiss it.

There are false teachings telling people they don't need to read the Old Testament because we have Yeshua. I love teaching God's Word, all of it. Yes, Yeshua replaced the sacrifice of animals. But He did not do away with the Torah, Prophets, or the writings of the Old Testament.

In Matthew 5:17, Yeshua says, *Do not think I have come to abolish the Law or the Prophets; I have not come to abolish them but fulfill them.* The word *fulfill* used in this verse can mean to *give true meaning*.[6] Yeshua came to help us understand or explain the true meaning of the Law and the Prophets. The Prophets are the Old Testament books of Joshua, Judges, 1 and 2 Kings, 1 and 2 Samuel, Isaiah, Jeremiah, and most of the books from Ezekiel to Malachi.

In Hebrews 10, we will see the author repeat many of the same themes we have read already. He is pushing the point of the uselessness of the Law to bring salvation. Remember, the people this author wrote to were turning back to Judaism because of pressure and persecution from the orthodox Jews.

To Obey is better than Sacrifice

Let's start reading **Hebrews 10:1-4.**

According to verse 1, what will the sacrifices of the law never accomplish?

_____

If the law had accomplished this, what would have ceased?

_____
_____

What is impossible according to these verses?

_____

Please read **Hebrews 10:5-10.**
Look in your Bible study notes or your cross-references in the margin of your Bible if you have them.
What Old Testament Scriptures do verses 5 through 7 come from?

_____

Go to those verses and read them. Does your Bible tell you who wrote these verses?

_____

You should notice a difference between the Old and New Testament renderings of these verses. It is God's Word and the writer of Hebrews knew what he was doing when he translated the verses from Hebrew to Greek. The passage's meaning is not lost.

In verse 5, to whom does the writer of Hebrews attribute these words?

_____

According to these verses, how did God look on the sacrifices?

_____

David used the verses from Psalm 40 to describe himself, but they describe Yeshua like many other verses in the Psalms. Since David was the ancestor of Yeshua, God promised to set up His kingdom forever through David's offspring (2 Sam. 7:12-17).

In **Hebrews 10:7, 9**, what did Yeshua come to do?

_____

At the end of verse 9, what does the author mean when he says, *He does away with the first in order to establish the second?*

_____

In verse 10, what did God's will achieve?

_____

Once. For. All. Unlike the blood of bulls and goats, which the priests sacrificed yearly on Yom Kippur for the sins of Israel, Yeshua's blood needed to be shed only once. Yeshua did away with the first covenant to set up the second, but He did away with the sacrifices and offerings to institute God's will for His people through His obedience.

I believe God wants a relationship with us more than anything else. But our obedience is important, too. In **1 Samuel 15:22-23**, Saul disobeyed God's commands, so God rejected Saul as king of Israel. The prophet Samuel told Saul, *Has the LORD as great delight in burnt offerings and sacrifices, as obeying the voice of the LORD? Behold, to obey is better than sacrifice, and to listen than the fat of rams.*

Obedience is how we show our love to God. He does not want us to work our fingers to the bone for Him unless He calls us to do it. If He calls us to rest, then we should be obedient to what He says. All the sacrifices we make of our time and efforts (busyness) or all the money and offerings we give in His name will not please God as much as our obedience to Him.

Golden Diamond - Day Two
The divine nature of Yeshua, glory and faith of the saints

The Footstool

Growing up, I lived on a farm with my parents and sisters. Every summer, we had house, garden, and yard work to do. My mom grew and canned our food, so it was our job to help her. Every time we complained, or she caught us sitting on the job, she said, "You can sit when you're done with your work!" That is just what we did. In the evening, we sat and watched our favorite TV shows and ate ice cream or a homemade snack with our parents; my mom's feet were up on her footrest and my dad reclined in his chair as we lay on the floor or couch. We will see what Yeshua did once He completed His work in this section of Hebrews 10.

Let's turn our attention to **Hebrews 10:11-14**. Please read these verses. Note in verses 11 and 12, the author made two distinctions.

What did the priest do daily?

_____

In my Bible, a number one is after *Christ* in verse 12. It signifies the Greek manuscripts said *this one* instead of *Christ*.

Why do you think the original Greek said *this one* instead of Christ?

_____

_____

What did Yeshua do after His sacrifice?

_____

_____

Hebrews 1:3, 1:13, 8:1, and 12:2 quote parts of verses 12 and 13, but it came from **Psalm 110:1**. Please go to Psalms and read it there.

Why do you think the author quoted parts of Psalm 110:1 in Hebrews so much?

_____

_____

_____

Just as my family sat after all our work was done for the day, I believe Yeshua did, too. Once the work of His earthly ministry and the cross was completed, He sat next to His Father. His work is done. Finished. Yeshua will have His own ottoman, too.

We can see this clearly in **Genesis 2:1-3**.

What words and phrases are repeated in Genesis 2:1-3?

_____

_____

According to Jewish tradition, God finished creating everything when He spoke these words. That means every soul that would ever be born or conceived was created at this time. This makes a lot more sense when we read **Jeremiah 1:5**: *Before I formed you in the womb, I knew you, and before you were born I consecrated you...*

In verse 14, what did Yeshua's offering do?

_____

_____

The word *perfected* used in verse 14 is the same Greek word used in Hebrews 10:1. One other meaning of the word *perfected is to bring to fruition.*[7] Fruition means the state of bearing fruit.[8] It's what God wants us to do. Yeshua's offering enables fruit to grow in our lives. As we are being made holy by the Holy Spirit, we bear fruit. Galatians 5:22 lists the fruit, which shows perfecting is taking place in our lives.

Forgiveness

Please turn to and read **Hebrews 10:15-18**. Verses 16 and 17 come from Jeremiah 31, which we read in Hebrews 8:8-12.

According to **Hebrews 10:15**, who said these verses?

_____

Remember, Jeremiah 31 records the New Covenant, which includes the Holy Spirit.

How does the Holy Spirit *bear witness* to us? To what does He bear witness?

_____

_____

Where are God's laws placed according to **Hebrews 10:16**?

_____

_____

Now look at **Hebrews 10:17** and compare it to **Hebrews 8:12b**. What differences do you see between these two verses?

_____

_____

You may wonder why the author added the words, "and their lawless deeds no more." Think about your answer for the question, "Where are God's laws placed..."

Where does sin originate within us?

_____

What is sin, according to God?

_____

Lawless deeds are things done outside the law of God. It is sin. The good news is God writes those same laws on our minds and places them on our hearts when we come to Yeshua. The Holy Spirit intervenes to remind us of them when sin tempts us to follow it.

Please go to **Mark 7:14-23**. What defiles us?

_____

Where do those things come from?

_____

This is why God places His laws on our hearts and minds. The Word of God reminds us of the righteous ways we should live and act. It fills your mind so the Holy Spirit can bring it to light in your heart and use it in your mind when you need it.

Golden Diamond - Day Three
The divine nature of Yeshua, glory and *faith of the saints*

My husband comes from a nice Greek family. His parents raised him right, but he wanted to be rich. That desire plunged him into a not-so-nice-world of people with the same mindset.

One summer, his then-girlfriend became a Christian while visiting her out-of-state family. Mike could tell she was different from their phone conversations. He devised a plan to "rescue" her from this "cult."

He flew out to be with her and to hang out with her friends and family. But God had devised a plan to rescue him as well. That Sunday, Mike went to church with her. It seemed to Mike the pastor wrote the sermon just for him. His girlfriend, her friends, and family had been praying for him the entire week before he got there, too. During the altar call, Mike made his way to the front of the church and accepted Yeshua as his Savior. Having a Christmas and Easter church experience, he didn't have the slightest idea what to do next.

He flew home and looked for a church.

On the plane ride back to Ohio, Mike realized God had changed his life forever. The day after returning home, he shared Yeshua with a friend. What amazed him most was how the Word of God flowed out of his mouth as he witnessed to this man. He had not memorized Scripture, much less read it, yet he spoke with authority, knowing the words were not his own.

God placed His Word in Mike's heart and mind when he came to Yeshua. It was the Holy Spirit's anointing that enabled him to share the life-giving words found only in Yeshua to another.

He and his girlfriend broke up soon after that. Years later, Mike and I married.

Hebrews 10:18 tells us great news. First, he says, *Where there is forgiveness of these...* What are "these"? _____

There is no longer any offering for sin.

The single offering of Yeshua's blood was more than enough to claim forgiveness for every sin. We only need to repent. It's so easy, yet so hard. Unfortunately, pride and unbelief keep us from God's forgiveness. Approaching the throne of mercy and grace is all we must do to find forgiveness because it exists there in heavenly truck loads. Ephesians 1:7-8 tells us God lavishes His grace on us.

Leviticus 4:1 explains the sacrifice of a lamb, goat, or bull only provided forgiveness for unintentional sins. Intentional sins, like lying, stealing, idolatry, adultery, slander, or murder, needed to be repented of, plus they came with a penalty of punishment or death.

What has pride or unbelief kept you from? Give it to Yeshua. He wants to forgive and extend His grace to you.

_____

_____

The New Way

Next, let's read **Hebrews 10:19-25**. This passage begins with *Therefore*. This word refers to the context of Jeremiah 31 and the forgiveness of sin. The author uses the word *since* (or *having* in some translations) twice and *let us* three times in these verses. Let's look at these phrases first. Write down the two *since* or *having* phrases. (Note: don't worry about writing every word of each phrase; get the main idea of it.)

1)._____

2)._____

In the first phrase, we find the words: *The Holy places*. Keep in mind this incorporates the Holy place and the Most Holy place. The curtain separating the Holy place from the Holy of Holies represents Yeshua's flesh. On Yom Kippur, the high priest splattered the blood from the bull and goat onto the curtain. When God tore the curtain in two after Yeshua's death, it mirrors His body torn for us.

Now, what are the *Let us* phrases? Again, you do not have to write every word of the phrase.

1)._____

2)._____

3)._____

Why can we do these three things?

_____

Please think about the *Let us* phrases. Which of these might you consider difficult? Can you draw near to God in faith? Is your hope wavering? Or do you doubt God's promises or faithfulness? Do you find it difficult to stir others up to love and produce good works? If any of these are challenging, commit them to prayer. Record a prayer here or in a journal.

_____

Let me paraphrase **Hebrews 10:19-24** for you….

Because we have forgiveness of sin through Yeshua's blood, we can be confident entering the Holy Places. It is a new and living way He opened for us. Because we have a Great High Priest interceding for us in Heaven, we can come to Him in faith, knowing He cleansed our evil hearts with His blood and made our bodies clean. Without wavering, we can confess our belief in the One who holds our hope, our faithful promise keeper. Now, let's think of ways to provoke others to love and do good works.

Verses 24 and 25 go together, but verse 25 gives a command. What is it?

_____

He gives a motivation to encourage each other, too. What is it?

_____

Golden Diamond - Day Four
The divine nature of Yeshua, glory and faith of the saints

As our world and culture grow more evil and our time gets shorter, we need each other more. It is important to stay in fellowship with one another to support and help each other through hard times. I admit a few of the trials I had were because of the church I attended. But other times I don't know what I might have done without my church.

When my twins were born, they were thirteen weeks premature. It was devastating. We were not sure they could live. When the hospital released me, I had to leave without my babies. It was one of the worst days of my life. We had friends praying and even the church I lived next to but didn't attend came over and offered prayer and support. I had a cesarean-section and could not drive for six weeks. The women of my church volunteered to drive me to and from the hospital to see my babies. It was a forty-five-minute drive one way.

On one occasion, my daughter was having a terrible day. While I was visiting, her lungs collapsed. She was already on a ventilator, but the neonatal staff could not keep her lungs inflated. She was so weak and gray-looking because of the lack of oxygen circulating in her tiny body. My driver, who I met for the first time that day, was eight months pregnant, and had three other children at home. I knew she needed to go, but I could not leave Alexandria. I told her to leave me there, but she would not go. She stayed with me until my baby girl was stable. My husband was at our restaurant and since this sister did not want me to be alone at home, she took me there. I don't see her anymore but will always remember this woman's kindness and the care she and the other women who took me back and forth to the hospital gave me for six weeks.

We found out at 4 a.m. the next morning, Alexandria had pneumonia in both lungs, and they listed her in critical condition. She was and is a fighter. She graduated from college recently.

Describe a time in your life when you needed your church. What was happening in your life at the time, and how did the church's response make you feel?

_____
_____
_____
_____
_____

The Hands of the Living God

Please read **Hebrews 10:26-31**. Up until now, we see a forgiving, loving God who sent His only Son to die for us. We understand God wants our best and will do everything He can to draw us to Him. However, in these verses we are going to see another side of God. This is the fourth of five warnings in the book of Hebrews.

The first exhortation was found in Hebrews 2:1. It warned us against *drifting away* from what we have heard. The second was found in Hebrews 3:7-19. Here, the author warns us about a heart issue of *unbelief*--not believing what you have been told. The third warning comes from Hebrews 5:11-12. It focuses on the *dullness of hearing* or *laziness* of studying and reading the Word.

What is the fourth exhortation the author gives us in **Hebrews 10:26**?

_____
_____

Let's explore the words of this verse more. It is not talking about the sin we may struggle with or even constant temptation we may experience. The word *deliberately* means "willingly, purposely, intentionally."[9] This is what we call apostasy. Apostasy means, "A falling away, a withdrawal, a defection."[10] It is a heart condition. This happens when someone receives and accepts the truth but turns away from it. Once we accept Yeshua as our Savior, God places His law on our hearts and writes it on our mind. God gives us His Holy Spirit to show and teach us the ways of God. But we go against everything God has put in us.

The author is showing a progression within these exhortations. First, we drift away by not paying close attention to what God's Word teaches us. Then, we doubt what we hear and read, which leads to unbelief. From there, we may not read or study our Bibles anymore. Going to church may become a thing of the past, too. Finally, we get to a point where we don't care about our sin. We reject truth. We are disobedient.

What does the phrase, "There no longer remains a sacrifice for sins" mean? I believe it means Yeshua's sacrifice does not cover the sin of deliberate rejection of truth. Does this mean God will not take us back when we humble ourselves and repent with genuine remorse? *No.* God loves a humble heart! He will always forgive someone possessing humility and remorse. But this is not who we are speaking of. I am talking about an arrogant, rebellious rejection of the truth of God. It is possible for a Christian to get to this point from the steps we outlined above. It may only start with a drifting away…

When a sacrifice no longer exists for sin, verse 27 tells us what to expect. What is it?

_____

_____

Please read **Hebrews 10:28-31**. Verse 28 comes from **Deuteronomy 17:1-7**. Let's look at those verses, too. Deuteronomy 17 refers to the first commandment: *You shall have no other gods before me* (Ex. 20:3). The Pharisees and scribes stoned those caught breaking this commandment, as long as there were two or more witnesses. The author of Hebrews compares this law and committing apostasy against the Son of God.

The author gives three characteristics of a person who deserves punishment in verse 29. What are they?

_____

_____

_____

The first words we will look at are *spurned* or *trampled on*. Both words come from the Greek word *katapateō* meaning "despise, show utter disdain."[11] Those are intense words. Let's keep going, then we will stop and consider what we read. The next word is *profaned*. This comes from the Greek word which means "worthless, of little value."[12] Lastly, the word *outraged* means "to insult."[13]

According to verse 29, what did the blood of the covenant do for the one who, now, goes on sinning? _____

This verse is referring to a believer; one God sanctified.

Golden Diamond - Day Five
The divine nature of Yeshua, glory and *faith of the saints*

"You'll never amount to a hill of beans." My mother's parents often directed this hurtful insult at some of their children. It affected my mom all her life, leaving her to believe the lie that she was worthless. How many insults have you believed? Yeshua knew better than to believe words like those, He knew who He was and the love His Father had for Him. Words that tear down and leave us feeling insignificant and wounded are always from the accuser. Ask the Holy Spirit to heal and speak truth into your heart.

In **Hebrews 10:29**, the words *despise (spurned)* and *worthless (profaned)* refer to Yeshua while *insult (outrage)* refers to the Holy Spirit. Turn to **Mark 3:22-30**. In this story, you see the scribes accusing Yeshua of healing by Satan's power. Yeshua tells them, "How can Satan cast out Satan?"

In verse 29, Yeshua delivers a stern warning.
What is it?

_____

_____

What Yeshua says to these scribes is this: If you give credit to Satan for what the Holy Spirit does, you will not be forgiven for such a sin. They accused Yeshua of having an unclean spirit in Him. God is serious about what we say concerning His Son and Spirit.

Despising Yeshua, considering His blood worthless, and insulting the Holy Spirit are serious sins against the Godhead.

Look how verse 29 describes the Spirit. What is His name?

_____

We can describe grace as unmerited favor. To insult Someone so powerful, yet who shows us unmerited favor... well, what can we say?

If you have a child who serves in the military or has given his or her life for this country, I thank you. But imagine despising them for their career choice or finding their sacrifice for our freedom worthless! Unfortunately, this has happened to great men and women of our armed forces. Think how you might react if this were your child? What parent can tolerate the slandering of their respectable son or daughter? God is no different. To have one of His own turn on His Son, who gave everything for us, hurts and angers God.

Re-read **Hebrews 10:30-31**.

What is God's reaction to this apostasy in these verses?

_____

_____

When our heart is in this state, it can be a fearful thing. We cannot take God for granted. He is the all-powerful, all-knowing Creator. He loves us, unconditionally. But He is just. He cannot tolerate deliberate, rebellious acts against Him. I am not implying God kills people, but He can and does discipline us. But, most importantly, God forgives us when we turn our hearts back to him. **2 Peter 3:9** says, *The Lord is not slow to fulfill his promise as some count slowness, but is patient toward you, not wishing that any should perish, but that all should reach repentance.*

The Promise

Hebrews 10:32-39 sets the stage for chapter 11. In this passage, we see what the author's audience endured. The author wants them to remember the days after their *enlightenment*, or the time they came to Yeshua.

Record what their life was like after they came to Christ.

_____
_____
_____
_____
_____

We can see they were tightly knit, too. What was their attitude like during this time?

_____
_____

Most of us have never been exposed to this kind of persecution. Let's face it, we have it pretty good for now. Imagine being treated as they were. Could you stay faithful to Yeshua?

In verse 35, the author tells them not to throw away, or do away with, their confidence. The Greek word means *courage* or *boldness*.[14] This confidence will have a great reward. But, they have given in to fear.

In verse 36, what do they need? _____

For what reason?

_____

Think about what we, who are in Christ, are promised. Turn to **James 1:12**.

What has God promised us if we *endure*?

_____

Fear can keep us from doing God's will. The *fear of rejection* says, "What if others don't like me or want me around because I am doing what God called me to do?" While the *fear of man* says, "What if people leave my church or Bible study because I am not doing it their way but God's way?" It is easier to do things our way or the way others want us to. But there is a reward for doing God's will and following Him no matter what people may say or do.

A portion of **Hebrews 10:37-38** quotes from Habakkuk 2:4. Here the *coming one* refers to the Messiah. If you think about it, every generation since Yeshua ascended to Heaven has waited and hoped for His return to take place in their generation.

What does God want us to do in verse 38?

_____

The Bible Exposition Commentary says, "We are not just saved from our sin by faith; we also must live by faith."[15] This is so true. We need faith to be saved, but we need faith to live the life God has called us.

Since God is omniscient, He can't be surprised. But it doesn't mean He will approve of our actions. He wants us to obey Him. He doesn't want us to shrink back or avoid doing what He tells us to do. That is disobedience. *Growing and maturing is changing how we respond to God.* This is why He is patient with us.

Hebrews 10:39 should be our mantra:
We are not those who shrink back and waste our life,
but those who have faith and preserve our souls.

1 Peter 1:7 (NLT) says:
These trials are only to test your faith, to show it is strong and pure. It is being tested as fire tests and purifies gold — and your faith is far more precious to God than mere gold. So, if your faith remains strong after being tried by fiery trials, it will bring you much praise and glory and honor on the day when Jesus Christ is revealed to the whole world.

What spoke to you in Hebrews 10? What nuggets of gold did God show you about your faith?

_____
_____
_____

Chapter 11 – Lapis Lazuli
Heaven, revelation, priesthood, and *the Jehovah Color*

Day One

The lapis lazuli is a blue, opaque stone with pyrite, or fool's gold, running through it. Although you may not see it around the neck of a queen or a famous actress, that does not mean people don't wear it in necklaces, rings, and earrings. Ancient civilizations prized and sought after this stone for jewelry, pottery, and statues. The Egyptians used it for the eyebrows of the famous King Tut mask and powdered it for eyeshadow.[1]

The Italian painter, Cennino Cennini called lapis "the most perfect color" because of its lovely blue hue. Thirteenth and fourteenth century artists ground it and used it for paint. During the Middle Ages, only the rich owned these stones.[2]

The Ancient Romans called it a sapphire, so most biblical references to the sapphire mean the lapis lazuli. Mined in Afghanistan, among other places, its name comes from the Persian word *lazward*, which means blue.[3] Its color represents *Heaven, revelation, priesthood,* and the *Jehovah Color.* [4]

I know Hebrews 11 is the obvious choice to be the gold chapter, but that would have been too easy. Besides, I love the gold lapis has trickling through it since faith runs through this chapter, too. It has stories of real people who encountered God in marvelous ways yet lived and died not always knowing what they were doing or why and rarely saw the fulfillment of God's promises. But they continued in their faith and pursued God with all their hearts.

My first professional job out of college was working in a histology lab. Histology is the study of tissue, like stomach, heart, intestinal, lymph, or any other tissue found in the human body. If you have had surgery to remove a gallbladder, tumor, skin tag, or any other flesh, then it went to a histology lab, where a lab tech made it into a slide for the pathologist to examine under a microscope.

Working there was an experience that took a long time to heal from. My lab consisted of three people: one supervisor and one other histology lab tech, and I was the newest and youngest. Both other women had been working in this lab *for years*. I came in, excited to learn with my new BS degree in biology, which would be used against me later. Unfortunately, my supervisor did not like me from the get-go, and I believe her goal was to make my life and job miserable.

At twenty-five years old, I had a stomach ulcer, which made it tough to eat without pain. I cried to the Lord every single day on my way to work. It was a hellish place. Discouragement and hopelessness were my constant companions, it seemed. After a year, I interviewed for a job on another floor of the hospital. They offered me the position, but I had **no** peace. I knew the Lord did not want me to take that job. Saddened, I turned it down, but afterward, I had immediate peace. Once I had been there for two years, the lab manager gave me a significant pay raise and promotion because of my degree and experience. My supervisor, who had no control over this, and the other histology tech, were furious. They stopped talking to me and increased the attacks, wanting to prove I was undeserving of this promotion. At this point, I begged God to let me leave. He did.

During those two years, the Lord surrounded me with praying friends and mentors who taught me a lot about prayer and spiritual warfare. I knew the Lord was with me. After I quit, the Lord had an incredible job waiting for me in cancer research. They were looking for a histologist with two years of lab experience. If I had taken my eyes off Yeshua and given in to the hopelessness of my circumstances, I would have missed out on a job I loved.

Faith

Read **Hebrews 11:1,** and in your own words, record the meaning of faith.

_____

_____

Oswald Chambers said, "Faith is deliberate confidence in the character of God whose ways you may not understand at the time."[5]

Let's look at some words from Hebrews 11:1 in Greek.
1. **Assurance**–the Greek word is *hypostasis,* which has two parts to it.
The first is *hypo* which means "of by, with and under."[6] The second is *histemi* which means "to abide, continue, establish, hold up, lay, present, set (up), stand (by, forth, still, up)."[7] We can read the word assurance as "to continue under or stand with or by (God)."[8]

The second part of this word, *histemi* is used in **Ephesians 6:11** as *stand*. Please turn to and read that verse.

What are we to stand against in this verse?

_____

Stand or *histemi* is an active position. It means to continue or abide. You can think of it as continuing to keep our eyes on the Lord or abiding in Christ no matter what is going on around us. We are not inactive; we are standing.

2. **Conviction**–the Greek word is elegchos meaning a *proof* or *test*.[9] Faith is our proof of things not seen.
Hebrews 11:1 could be read as: Faith is continuing with God (trust) for things hoped for and the proof of things not seen. Faith is trusting God and standing regardless of our circumstances. *It's believing God when you can't see what He is doing.*
Read verse 2.

Who are the people of old or the ancients?

_____

How did God measure how godly or righteous they were?

_____

Look at verse 3 through the lens of Creation vs. Evolution. How would you explain this to someone?

_____

_____

_____

We cannot see faith any more than we can prove Creation to a non-believer. All things were created by the word of God. He spoke, and it came into being. When God wanted to create water, He spoke the molecules of hydrogen and oxygen to form bonds that would make it. This is hard for a Bible-believing Christian to comprehend, let alone a non-believer.

Faith is what sets us apart from everyone else.

On a scale of one to ten, (one is low and ten is high) how is your faith? Why? Is there an area where your faith is struggling? In what area is your faith thriving?

_____

_____

God is the only One who needs proof of our faith. Keep abiding in Yeshua. He will hold you up when you need it.

We are going to read the stories of many "people of old." The author shared these accounts to demonstrate the struggles of real people whom God considered righteous. God knew their struggles, and He knows ours. He is sympathetic to our plight.

Walking with God

Turn to and read **Hebrews 11:4**. The author starts with Abel.

What does this verse say about Abel's sacrifice?

_____

Let's go back to Genesis to read his story.
Genesis 4:1-6 tells the story referred to in Hebrews 11:4. Please read it.

What did Abel bring?

_____

What did Cain bring?

_____

If you are anything like me, you have heard plenty of sermons on this passage or read commentaries about it. What was so special about Abel's offering over Cain's? We may even look at this passage and think, why did God treat Cain this way? Let's take a closer look at Abel's offering.

Genesis 4:4 says, *And Abel brought of the firstborn of his flock and of* their *fat portions.* I emphasized the word *their* for a reason. In English, the word *their* is a neutral pronoun. We can say, their dishes, their socks, their dog, and out of context we don't know the gender of the people spoken of. In Genesis 4:4 we don't know the gender of the sheep referred to in our English Bibles. But pronouns in the Hebrew language are either feminine or masculine. The Hebrew word for *their* is *hen* and it is a feminine pronoun, which means the firstborn of Abel's flock were female lambs.

In the agricultural world, when your sheep, goats, or cows have females it means you can have more babies to grow your herd. You don't need a lot of males. We had one buck with our six or so females. In the animal world, males have two basic functions, and those are to breed and to guard his herd, and most of the time there is only one male per herd.

When a doe gives birth and we see it is a doeling, we rejoice! When a buck is born, we start thinking about selling or castrating him. If you have too many males, they fight. You need extra room to keep them separated from each other or your girls. In the Old Testament, most of the animals sacrificed were males: rams, bulls, and male goats or bucks. That was God's plan.

However, Abel brought his firstborn female lambs to God. It was truly a sacrifice and it was a better offering. God looked on Abel's sacrifice with favor and for that reason, "he still speaks."

Lapis Lazuli - Day Two
Heaven, revelation, priesthood, and *the Jehovah Color*

My oldest brother died when he was ten years old. I was just a baby, so I never knew him, but it nearly wrecked my mom and dad. My dad carried David's obituary in his Bible the rest of his life. Death is cruel. We don't understand why some die so young and others live so long.

My brother had a severe brain injury shortly after he was born (no fault of my parents). It caused blindness, cerebral palsy, and the inability to breathe on his own for the rest of his life, so he needed intense care. My parents had many other children and my dad started having major health problems shortly after David's death. I can't imagine my mom taking care of a very dependent child along with a husband who never worked again after turning fifty-six. I can see God's mercy in this situation, although I'm sure my parents didn't see it that way at first. God is sovereign. We know my brother was healed the moment the Lord took him to heaven.

Please read **Hebrews 11:5**. This portion is about Enoch. **Genesis 5:21-24** records his story. Read those verses, too.

What happened to Enoch?

_____

Why? _____

Genesis 5:22 says, "Enoch walked with God…" This phrase means Enoch pleased God. He walked closely and stayed near God, and for that reason Enoch never died a physical death. Maybe God "took" Enoch because of the growing evil in the world. We can only guess, really, since the Bible doesn't tell us why he disappeared.

Read **Hebrews 11:6**.

According to this verse, how do we please God? _____

If we want to draw near to God, what must we know and believe?

_____

Here are a few more verses that speak of drawing near to God. Record how each of these verses wants us to approach God.

Hebrews 10:22

_____

James 4:8

_____

_____

Psalm 145:18

_____

Obedience

Read **Hebrews 11:7** and Noah's story in **Genesis 6:5-9.**

How did God feel about Noah?

_____

How did God feel about the rest of the world?

_____

Read **Genesis 6:22**, **7:5**, and **7:16**. How did Noah respond to what God commanded of him?

_____

As a result of obedience in constructing the ark, what did Noah do to the world in **Hebrews 11:7**?

_____
_____

What did Noah become because of his faith? _____

In contrast to Noah's righteousness and obedience, the world was evil and rebellious. Even though rain had never fallen on the earth Noah believed in and obeyed God.

What would you have done if you were Noah? Building a boat for the sea is one thing. Building it for a coming flood in a region which has never seen rain, is another.

Is God telling you to build an "ark?" What is it? How are others responding to your "ark?"

_____
_____
_____

When God told me to write Bible studies, I laughed out loud! I had no desire to write, nor did I consider myself a writer. But I responded to His voice, using the studies to help and encourage others.

Read **Hebrews 11:8-12**. Have you ever felt called to go somewhere or do something but did not understand why or what you would do once you got there?

Has God ever told you to leave your hometown and family? Why? Where did you go?

_____
_____

If you answered yes to the above question, you can appreciate what Abram went through. God told him to leave his family and the only place he called home; the two things most valued. It was his identity, security, and wealth. People stayed in their family groups and traveled together. But God had other ideas.

Turn to **Genesis 12:1-3**.

After God told Abram to leave his home, what did God promise him?

_____
_____

In **Genesis 12:4-9**, where was Abram going? _____

What did God promise him there? _____

What was Abram's calling?

_____

Just like Abram, God has a calling on your life. It is bigger than you realize. God doesn't show us the big picture; we probably couldn't handle it. His path is seldom a straight line, but God's way will lead us to the place He wants.

If you're not aware of your calling, petition God for a view. Maybe you've become discouraged because of the time you spent "traveling" from one place to another; ask for encouragement. Pray together with a friend or family member who may feel the same way. Above all, be obedient. God will bless you for it.

Lapis Lazuli - Day Three
Heaven, revelation, priesthood, and *the Jehovah Color*

Foreigner in a Foreign Land

My dad had a stroke at fifty-six years old. He wasn't able to work again as a result of partial paralysis. He spent his days reading the Bible and in prayer. My dad loved God's Word and read it to us at the dinner table each evening, often weeping over the promises he found. He prayed for my sisters and me all the time, especially as we kneeled by his chair before bed. Dad wasn't perfect, and in a lot of ways the stroke changed his personality, but it also strengthened his faith. Now and then, he believed the lies of depression, telling him he was useless and a burden. His health declined until his death twenty-one years later. I was twenty-seven.

Reread **Hebrews 11:9-10**. In verse 9, depending on your translation, it says, *By faith he [Abram] went to live…* In the Greek, it means "to live as a foreigner."[10] Abram was an alien in a foreign land.

What was he looking forward to?

_____

_____

In your own words, what was Abram expecting from God?

_____

_____

Abram knew God was laying a foundation to build upon. The definition of *foundation* according to Merriam-Webster is "a body or ground upon which something is built up or overlaid."[11] Abram trusted in his Architect. Do you?

God has been laying a foundation in your life since the day of your conception. He blessed you with gifts and talents to use in your calling. We read about this in Chapter 3. Yeshua is our builder.

Turn to **Ephesians 2:19-22**. These verses are similar to Hebrews 11:9-10.

Who are the aliens and foreigners in these verses?

_____

Who or what is the foundation? _____

These verses add Yeshua as the Cornerstone. According to *Wikipedia.com*, the cornerstone is "the first stone set in the construction of a masonry foundation, important since all other stones will be set in reference to this stone, thus determining the position of the entire structure."[12] Yeshua is the Cornerstone who determines the position of His Church. Without Him, we will crumble.

In Abram's time, God was building him into a nation to be the foundation for the gospel. Our Messiah came out of this nation to build His Church, in which the sons and daughters of Abram would be the first missionaries. When God called Abram, he saw Mary, the disciples, Paul, Timothy, and many others who would live and die for Him. He also saw you and me. He knew our part in His plan before time. (Eph. 1:3-4.)

In **Hebrews 11:11**, how is Sarah's faith described?

In **Genesis 18:9-15**, we read how Sarah laughed when God told Abraham she would have a son in a year. Unfortunately, this is the picture most of us have of her. But Hebrews says she considered God and His promise faithful.

How is Abraham described **in Hebrews 11:12**?

_____

Abraham was 100 years old when Sarah had Isaac (Gen. 21:5). Yet, all twelve tribes of Israel are counted as His children, as well as all those who have ever known Yeshua as their Savior. Billions. His descendants number as many as the stars in heaven and the grains of sand by the seashore.

Is there something God's asked you to do, yet you feel too old to start over or to start something new? This is exactly how I felt when God prompted me to write my first Bible study in my forties. Now, I am in my fifties writing this Bible study, thinking why couldn't I have started this thirty years ago? Why in the world did God give me a brand-new skill to learn now? I look around and see many young women leading ministries, writing books, and having huge followings. Who will care what I have to say and write?

I must trust God has a purpose for this study and for wanting a novice to write it. I must stop looking in the mirror, wishing to see a young woman instead of a middle-aged woman, and trust God's plan for my life.

Little did I know, but this Bible study is the "child" I have wanted for a long time.

Maybe you are asking God for an actual child, or maybe some other kind of "child."

What aspirations have you been dreaming of but feel too old to achieve or do?

_____

_____

Hebrews 11:13 lists four acts of faith that describe the people we have talked about so far. Record each point you find in this verse. Your Bible translation may be slightly different and have more or less than four, don't worry about it.

1. _____

2. _____

3. _____

4. _____

These people, and millions more like them, have died believing what God told them.

My dad prayed over my sisters and me each night as we knelt by his knee. He read God's Word every evening before dinner while we sat around the table. After his stroke, my father did not understand why, but God knew the influence he would have on my life.

Every day he looked from afar at the promises God gave, knowing His Word does not come back void. As a stranger in a foreign land waiting for his true Home, he loved God and longed for the day he'd see Him face to face.

I pray there is someone like this in your life. If not, be that person for someone else.

Hebrews 11:14-16 continues describing these saints. Let these words sink into your heart and soul. They are examples of godly men who loved and trusted God. Verse 16 makes me want to weep!

What were they seeking? _____

At any time, what could they have done? _____

What did they desire? _____

God is not ashamed to be called their God. These words! A perfect and powerful God is not ashamed of these imperfect and weak men.

My dad often felt useless as he watched us girls do the work he once did in the yard and garden. He suffered from depression and even tried to take his life once. But God was not ashamed of him, nor was He embarrassed to be his God.

Despite our struggles, our wavering faith, and even our lack of trust, God is not ashamed to be called our God. He loves you and has prepared a place for you. Keep believing, keep trying, and keep following Him. If you ever feel like a stranger or an alien, you are in good company.

As great as your town, state, or country may be, it is not your home. God made you for a better place.

Lapis Lazuli - Day Four
Heaven, revelation, priesthood, and *the Jehovah Color*

Blessings

As I shared in Chapter 4, during the Shabbat meal, parents took time to bless their children while holding their faces in their hands and praying words of scripture over them. This is a tradition that goes back to the days of Moses. It's not that popular today, at least in the American culture. I picture God doing that with each of His children. We may not feel His two hands holding our faces tenderly, but if you listen closely, you might just hear His gentle voice speaking a blessing over you.

Please read **Hebrews 11:17-22**. Here we see everyone from Abraham to Joseph mentioned.

In verses 17-19, how did Abraham demonstrate his faith in God?

_____

In verse 20, how did Isaac express his faith in God?

_____

Hebrews 11:21-22 tells us Jacob blessed the sons of Joseph (**Gen. 48**) and Joseph directed his brothers to take his bones back to Canaan, the land of Abraham, Isaac, and Jacob, when they left Egypt (**Gen. 50:22-26**).

Hebrews 11:20-21 says blessings came from the father or grandfather to his sons. You can read these blessings in the Genesis chapters I have in highlighted in bold above.

Why do you think it took *faith* to make these blessings?

_____

_____

In **Hebrews 11:22**, why do you think it took *faith* for Joseph to give instructions concerning the Exodus and his bones?

_____

_____

Turn to **Mark 11:22-24**. In your own words, what is faith, according to this verse?

_____

_____

How do the verses in Mark relate to the blessings of Isaac and Jacob and the directions of Joseph?

_____

_____

The Greek word for *faith* is *pistis*. This word means "what can be believed, a state of certainty regarding belief, trust, believe to a complete trust."[13] Faith is equal to trust. It is trusting God with your past, present, and future. Abraham, Isaac, Jacob, and Joseph trusted God with their future generations.

It's difficult for most of us to think about the future beyond our own children. Joseph reflected on his descendants and the time they would leave Egypt. He was looking (although he didn't know how far) 400 years into the future. We can't comprehend that. When I was growing up, my grandmother, aunts, uncles, and parents told us *the Lord will return any day*. I'm not sure if they ever looked past this impending reality and guessed Yeshua may not come back as soon as they assumed. If they had, I think their lives would have been different.

If we focus on the world as we know it ending within our lifetime, we will not look ahead to the world we may leave our grandchildren and great-grandchildren. Our behavior will lack responsibility for the world we leave our future sons and daughters or grandchildren.

Abraham, Isaac, Jacob, and Joseph looked ahead at the nation God would make out of their descendants. They believed God had a plan and purpose for them and believed what God told them. Therefore, they could pray future blessings over their children. This is a Hebrew custom. I am not sure how many other countries or ethnic groups speak blessings over their children's lives, but it is not an American thing. Praying over our children is not what I am not talking about. I am referring to placing your hands on your children and blessing them, their potential spouse and family, and their future.

This is an example we need to incorporate into our children's lives.

Are you focused on the world you live in today, or the one to come? What are ways we can help change the future for our descendants?

_____
_____
_____

What blessings can you pray over your children, grandchildren, or other young people in your life?

_____
_____

Moses–A Life of Faith

Hebrews 11:23-29 is mostly about Moses' life. We have read a lot about Moses through this book. In this next section, we will see how much faith was a part of his life.

How did faith touch his life before he was even aware?

_____

Please read **Exodus 1:15-22.** Before Moses' birth, God was preparing a way for him.

How did the midwives demonstrate faith?

_____

Both **Exodus 2:1-22,** told by Moses himself, and **Acts 7:20-29,** told by Stephen to the high priest and council, tell the story of Moses' birth, his time in Egypt, and his escape to the land of Midian. Please read both sections to enrich the Hebrews 11 passage. The account of Moses in Exodus may be a little different from the one in Acts and Hebrews, but maybe there's more to the story than Moses wrote.

Moses had a very extravagant life in Pharaoh's palace. Despite what modern movies have led us to believe, it appears Moses knew who his people were while living with Pharaoh's daughter. He had compassion on them, even from his life of luxury.

In **Hebrews 11:24-25**, what choices did Moses make?

Why did he make these decisions?

Verse 26 may seem a little out of place when referring to Moses and the time he lived. Obviously, Yeshua did not "live" during Moses' time as He did in the New Testament. As we discussed earlier in this study, I believe Moses met and spoke with Yeshua on different occasions. The Hebrews author may make the point Moses was content to suffer for God's plan, knowing a salvation would take place through Him.

Please read **Hebrews 11:27-29**.

How is Moses' faith described in verse 27?

Turn to **1 John 4:18**. What does this verse say about fear?

Moses had no fear of Pharaoh while leaving Egypt. In fact, he kept his eye on the One he could not see. How crazy does that sound? While it is true, we cannot see God, Yeshua, or the Holy Spirit, we should know when They show up. Feeling Their Presence is as good as seeing Them.

Yeshua has been closest in my despair. The Holy Spirit speaks through me as I teach and write or drops thoughts into my mind, giving me direction, comfort, or correction. God speaks through His Spirit as He heals and changes me.

We should expect God to be present in our lives. Moses did. He did not fear his circumstances, because he saw an invisible God. He saw God by His works. Moses saw God in his answered prayers.

How do you "see" God in your life? How and when has He shown up?

According to **Hebrews 11:28**, how is Moses' faith demonstrated? Why is that considered faith?

Exodus 11-12 explain the tenth plague and the Passover. The tenth plague involved the death of Pharaoh's firstborn down to the firstborn of the livestock. The only way to avoid having your firstborn child or calf die was to put a lamb's blood on the doorposts of your home. At midnight, the Lord's destroyer struck down the firstborn throughout Egypt but passed over the houses covered by the blood.

Men and Women of Faith

Hebrews 11:29-30 is not about individuals as the other verses have been. **Exodus 14** tells the story of the crossing of the Red Sea, and **Joshua 6** tells the story of the walls of Jericho.

Who did the author include in each of these events, and why do you think these verses in Hebrews

11:29-30 are significant?

_____

_____

_____

Lapis Lazuli - Day Five
Heaven, revelation, priesthood, and *the Jehovah Color*

Following anyone requires faith. If you do not trust a person, you will not follow them. A righteous leader should abide by biblical principles and lead out of obedience and love for Yeshua. Most churches are only as godly as their pastor is, and a country is only as godly as its government. Strong, holy leadership in our churches will encourage people to step out in faith and follow the One who is leading their pastor. As our churches go, our communities, states, and country will follow.

We must put our faith in God and do as He says. To know what He says, we must read His Word.

Hebrews 11:31 speaks of Rahab, the woman who hid two of Joshua's spies when they went into Jericho to assess the land. Please read her story in **Joshua 2:1-21** and **6:25**.

Turn to **Matthew 1:1-6**. Whose genealogy is this? Why was Rahab's faith noteworthy?

_____

_____

In **Hebrews 11:32-38,** the author lists a few more Old Testament men, but he realizes there are too many to mention. He also describes ways in which they died.

First, what did some of these men do through faith?

_____

_____

_____

Hebrews 11:35 refers to the women in **1 Kings 17:17-24** and **2 Kings 4:18-37**.

Which prophets do the scriptures mention, and what did they do?

_____

We may not live to see a resurrection, but our God is in the business of bringing the dead back to life. Spiritual death is separation from God.

My parents tried to raise us in a Christian home, but that didn't guarantee everyone in my family would grow up to love and serve Yeshua. A few of my sisters were not serious about following God in their youth and didn't marry Christian spouses. As a result, some of their children live apart from God. The **good news** is we serve a God who loves the lost. Just as He brought the dead back to their mothers in the book of Kings, He can raise those we love to life in Him.

Write the names of those you know who need life from Yeshua. Pray for them with your Bible study group or right now by yourself.

_____

_____

Hebrews 11:35-37 lists the methods of persecution these godly men endured or by which they lost their lives. I can't even imagine!

Record how people treated these men of faith.

_____

In the United States, we are so far removed from the persecutions listed in Hebrews 11:35-37. However, around the world, people suffer and die for their faith in Yeshua. It's hard to imagine sneaking to church in the middle of the night or only being able to mouth the words to your favorite worship song for fear of being overheard. In America, we have not experienced the police pounding on our door at night to whisk us away to prison for believing in the Messiah. However, this is commonplace in many countries. The enemy tears families apart through captivity, torture, and death because of their faith in the Son of God.

Yeshua is dangerous to our enemy, and how powerful our testimony must be to others, if Satan needs to kill, steal, and destroy us. I've heard it said, "If Satan isn't bothering you, you aren't threating him." Do you want to be a nuisance to Satan or just get by?

Put on your armor and go fight. Stand up for those who are weak and unable to defend themselves. Speak up for truth. God is raising up warriors, and warriors fight on His behalf.

What did the author of Hebrews say about these people in verse 38?

Have you ever known anyone described this way? What an outstanding statement to make about a person or people. Spiritual giants may be the meekest and most humble people we know. They may not stand out in a crowd or seem impressive, but they know God intimately and have experienced His mercy and love so much it overflows from them.

A Better Place

Read an incredible passage in **Acts 5:17-42** about the apostles.

After all was said and done, how did they respond?

Read **Matthew 10:22**. What does Yeshua warn in these verses?

In **Matthew 5:11-12**, how are we to feel when people persecute us?

How does **Matthew 5:11-12** follow **Hebrews 11:35-40**?

So why are we surprised when people reject, mock, or desert us because of our faith? We should expect it. Throughout the Bible, many hated God's people for following Him or Yeshua.

What are the promises within the verses of **Hebrews 11:35-40**?

In the New International Version (NIV), **Hebrews 11:39-40** says, *These were all commended for their* *faith, yet none of them received what God promised. God had planned something better for us so that only together with us would they be made perfect.*

What were the people (these Old Testament saints) promised, but they did not receive?

_____

Do you realize God will perfect the Church with the saints mentioned throughout Hebrews 11 and many more not mentioned? Even though they did not die "in Christ" as we will, God counts their faith as righteousness, and they will receive the promise when He perfects them.

As I wrote this chapter, I had a sense of loneliness and discouragement, like a car driving the wrong way on a one-way street. There have been many things going on during the last month of writing where I felt disconnected from others. As I thought about it regarding this chapter, I couldn't help wondering how many of the people we read about felt this way during their lives. How many times were they hopeless or felt abandoned? When everyone was going one direction, God called them to go the other.

This is our life as Christians. Yeshua invites us to go against the flow of the world. This place is not our home; we are aliens and foreigners trying to point a hostile world to a loving yet invisible God.

Hebrews 11 uses the word "better" three times. When our life in this world is over, God will raise us to a better or **superior** life, in a **superior** country, by God's **superior** plan in Yeshua. That is fantastic news!

In *My Utmost for His Highest*, Oswald Chambers wrote, "Faith must be tested, because it can be turned into a personal possession only through conflict. What is your faith up against right now?"[14]

How would you answer his question?

_____

_____

How did the lapis lazuli connect to Hebrews 11?

_____

_____

What did the Lord teach you in this chapter? How can you apply this chapter to your life?

_____

_____

_____

Chapter 12 - Pink Diamond
Joy, healing, and *new life in Christ*

Day One

The Pink Legacy diamond is a rare, nearly nineteen-carat, Fancy Vivid Pink,[1] emerald-cut gem. Only one out of one million diamonds are found to have this quality.[2] The jeweled ring is set in platinum with two white diamonds.[3]

Found primarily in Australia, pink diamonds are free from impurities, unlike other colored stones. Some believe pink diamonds may be formed when additional intense pressure (from seismic activity) changed their molecular structure, producing defects such as a pink color.[4]

The pink hue of this jewel symbolizes *joy, healing,* and *new life in Christ.*[5]

As you start Hebrews 12 today, you may be under intense pressure that affects your very core. Remember you are free to concentrate on the joy or the chaos. Let the pressures of this life bring out the joy within you. The world may see your joy and think you are crazy or "defective." I want you to find the pink diamond hidden in this chapter so you, too, can experience joy, healing, and a new life in Christ.

Michael is my youngest and most strong-willed son. Of course, he got that from his father. Disciplining him was not always easy since I didn't always understand this child. I remember when he was ten months old; I asked the doctor what was wrong with my baby. He bit, screamed, and sat on top of his older twin siblings, refusing to let them up. Even when I nursed him, he bit me, then looked up and smiled when I gasped in pain.

Michael's strong will has served him well as a college student. No one leads Michael where he doesn't want to go, nor is he a follower. He thinks and reasons everything out.

Because of Michael's determination as a little boy, most things turned into a fight, with him kicking and screaming while I carried him from the library or the grocery store. One time when Michael was four, I went to the grocery with all three of my kids to pick up a few items before dinner. This store had a supervised playroom for children under six while their moms shopped. My twins loved it, but not Michael. He wanted to go shopping with me.

The bakery gave cookies to the kids, so as soon as Michael saw the bakery he asked for a cookie. I told him no since it was near dinner time.

He screamed throughout the entire store.

When people saw me in an aisle, they turned and went a different direction. I finally took everything out of my cart placing them on a nearby shelf. I picked up my other two kids, with Michael still crying and screaming for a cookie. Everyone was looking at us! He yelled all the way home, too.

As I pulled into the driveway, my husband came to the car, asking me why I was home so fast.

Exasperated, I said, "Your son!"

After I explained what had happened, Mike said, "I'll take care of him, you can go back to the store." Michael was an angel when I got home, even apologizing for his behavior.

Without discipline from my husband and me, he might have become a rebellious young man with no respect for authority. We had to teach Michael respect at a very young age—more so than my older two children, who were more complacent and easy-going.

I learned I had to be stronger than Michael was. He would not have respected me unless I won more than a few battles. He had to learn to surrender his young will to mine—not in a breaking-the-spirit-kind-of-way. My husband and I never wanted to break him; we wanted to teach him through discipline.

This chapter my not be your favorite by the time you are done with it. But please remember God disciplines us because He loves us *and* so He won't have to punish us forever. Think about that. I would rather God discipline me on this earth and in this lifetime than discipline me throughout *eternity*.

Endurance to the End

Let's read **Hebrews 12:1-2**. In Hebrews 11, we read about many of the patriarchs, some of whom were martyred for their faith in God. The first two verses in Hebrews 12 shifts to address our faith.

What is our faith compared to in verse 1? _____

Where are the witnesses? _____

The people spoken of in Hebrews 11 are the cloud of witnesses surrounding us. They have run the race called faith and had to deal with their own sin and unbelief. Whether or not those people can see us or know what we experience is debatable. The point is they have gone before us and have run a similar race to ours — probably an even more difficult one than most of us.

In verse 1, what is the first thing the author tells us to get rid of? _____

How is sin portrayed in this verse? _____

What weight do you carry?

_____

If you have been in a race, whether on a track or in a pool, you know any extra weight slows you down. Athletes want to be as streamlined and as weight-free as they can. Even a runner's shoes are lightweight.

I dated a bodybuilder for a very short time in college. One day he wanted to do something I liked, so we played a game of tennis. It was a short game. The weight of his muscles hindered him from being able to chase a ball across the court. He was strong, so he hit the ball out of the court. I could easily hit the ball past him, too. He excelled at his sport, but his heavy muscles did not make him a good tennis player. His body was not in the right shape for a fast-moving game like tennis.

In **Hebrews 12:1**, does the author make our race sound more like a sprint or marathon?

_____

The sprinter has a lot of body mass, with thick leg muscles for explosive power. Short legs give them bursts of speed over small distances. Their muscular arms work like pumps, increasing the velocity of their legs to propel them over the finish line.[6]

The marathon runner has less mass with long, lean muscles in their arms and legs. They are slow and steady runners built for prolonged distances. Their long strides cover more ground with fewer steps.[7]

In your Christian life, which runner describes you? Why?

_____

_____

According to this verse, how are we to run? _____

Are you a sprinter who takes off into something good, but the battle or challenge drains you? You put all you have into a ministry, relationship, or prayer, but if it doesn't go the way you wanted or hoped, you're done.

Or are you the marathon runner who is slow and steady, enduring the race? You expect the wins and losses. Neither the victory, nor the defeat, changes who you are or your race for the prize.

In a race, runners keep their eyes ahead of them, looking toward the finish line. According to **Hebrews 12:2**, what are we to keep our eyes on? _____

How does the author describe Yeshua in the *first part* of verse 2?

_____

Many of us have heard these words used to describe Yeshua. But how often do you think about what they mean? The New Living Translation calls Yeshua the *champion who initiates and perfects our faith* in Hebrews 12:2. In the King James Version, Yeshua is *the author and finisher*, while the New International Version says He is *the pioneer and perfecter of faith.*

The English Standard Version calls Yeshua "the founder and perfector of our faith." Without Yeshua, there would be no faith. He originated, founded, authored, and pioneered our faith. He is also the perfector of our faith. We saw the word *perfect* meant *completion*, so *perfector* means *the one who brings completion*.[8]

Do you know what that means for us? Yeshua is the one who will complete our faith. Our job is to endure the race, or to *never give up*. Our Christian "walk" is a long-distance race and we need to keep running, keeping our eyes on Yeshua. He will complete what He began.

What are some ways we can keep our eyes on Yeshua while in this race?

_____

_____

The next part of verse 2 in **Hebrews 12** looks familiar. Compare it to verse 1.

A race is set before us, what was set before Yeshua? _____

We are asked to endure the race, what did Yeshua endure? _____

If Yeshua could face the cross with *joy*, how do you think we should face the race set before us?

_____

That's hard to get our heads around, isn't it? It astounds me how Yeshua could face the cross with joy. I have a hard time facing the day with joy, let alone torture.

How different our lives would be if we could find the joy in our everyday life among the kids' messes, the pet messes, dinner, laundry, errands, bills, late bills, illnesses, growing older, and whatever else we are going through.

He faced it because He saw you and me. He saw our life and our eternity.

It gave Him joy to know His death would give us life.

Pink Diamond - Day Two
Joy, healing, and *new life in Christ*

Here's my prayer for you: Romans 15:13 (NIV), *May the God of hope fill you with all joy and peace as you trust in him, so that you may overflow with hope by the power of the Holy Spirit.*

Now take out the "you" in this verse and replace it with a "me" and "I." Make this your prayer. Rewrite it here or in a journal with "me" and "I."

_____

_____

_____

In **Hebrews 12:2**, how did Yeshua feel about the shame of the cross?

_____

Yeshua did not allow the contempt of a public, naked, and torturous death keep Him from going to the cross. Nor did He let that disgrace have control over Him. I believe there was a battle won at Gethsemane, a battle over shame, humiliation, sorrow, rejection, and fear, among others.

Shame keeps us from Yeshua's love and forgiveness. Satan wants us to stay in a place of embarrassment, humiliation, and dishonor. There is no line in the sand that, once crossed, God says, "You've gone too far now." He offers His forgiveness to all without cost.

My sister hid her alcoholism for twenty years because she was ashamed of her inability to control her drinking. One day she realized Yeshua wanted to trade her condemnation for freedom, her humiliation for healing, and her hopelessness for joy. Shame prevented her from finding healing and forgiveness sooner. It kept her in a prison.

Is shame keeping you from experiencing joy, freedom, and healing in your walk with Yeshua? Take this opportunity to confess anything you are keeping from Yeshua. Be willing to be transparent with Him. Find someone you trust to pray with and for you or journal it. Please don't hold back from the Lord. You **will** find freedom and healing when you ask. Consider these verses:

Isaiah 61:7: *Instead of your shame, there shall be a double portion; instead of dishonor they shall rejoice in their lot; therefore in their land they shall possess a double portion; they shall have everlasting joy.*

Psalm 22:5: *To you [God] they cried and were rescued; in you they trusted and were not put to shame.*

Psalm 34:18: *The Lord is near to the brokenhearted and saves the crushed in spirit.*

Psalm 51:17 (NLT): *The sacrifice you desire is a broken spirit. You will not reject a broken and repentant heart, O God.*

The very last part of **Hebrews 12:2** says, *...and [he] is seated at the right hand of the throne of God.* When Yeshua triumphed over sin and death, His reward was to take His place beside His Father. We read about that in Chapter 1.

Read **Ephesians 1:20, 2:4-6**. Both passages are referring to God, and notice they are in past tense, too.

What do these verses mean to you?

_____

As the Godhead is triune, so are we; we are body, soul, and spirit. We live where the Spiritual and Natural world collide. While our body is confined to this world, our spirit communes with God in His *heavenly places*. As believers in Christ, we are spiritually raised as citizens of His home. Our life is in this heavenly place. This is where we find our identity, our worth, our blessings (Eph. 1:3), and fight our battles (Eph. 6:12).

How can this change your outlook in your daily walk with Yeshua?

_____

_____

Be Encouraged

Endure. In **Hebrews 12:3**, we see this word for a third time. The "Him" mentioned in this verse is Yeshua from verse 2.

What did Yeshua *endure* in this verse?

_____

Why? _____

The Greek word behind weary is *kamnō*, which means to "become discouraged, or to grow weary to the soul."[9] Have you ever been wearied down to your soul? But, according to this verse, Yeshua endured hostility (or rebellion and defiance, especially verbal[10]) so we can persevere.

Yeshua never promised prosperity or that everyone would love us. In fact, it was the opposite. He told us because He suffered, we will; because people hated Him, they will hate us. He endured everything He did to be our example.

In **Hebrews 12:4**, the author states the Hebrews have not given their lives for their faith, yet. Have they struggled? *Yes, but not to the point of martyrdom.* In the United States, we are in a culture that is growing more and more hostile to real Christianity. Are we persecuted like other countries? No. Only time will tell how long that lasts. The faith of many has grown cold because we have it so easy.

Let's read **Hebrews 12:5-11**.

How do you feel about discipline?

_____

_____

Have you ever felt the Lord's discipline? If yes, what was it like?

_____

_____

Part of verse 5 and verse 6 come from **Proverbs 3:11-12**.

According to these verses, how should we feel about God's *punishment*? (As the word *discipline* means in this sentence).

_____

_____

The word *regard* or *make light*, means *despise* in verse 5. We are not to despise "the discipline of the Lord."

This can be a difficult subject. You may have a child, or you may have been the child who rebelled against punishment, discipline, and instruction. Love may not be what our children think of when we discipline them. When we are angry or frustrated, it's possible to get harsh and degrading with our children.

We cannot compare our earthly father's chastisement with that of our Heavenly Father. I realize there may be abusive situations some have suffered. So, I am not saying this lightly. When we can forgive those who were harsh and even abusive to us, we can learn how to accept our Father's correction. He does it out of love, not exasperation or evil.

God understands each one of us so well. He knows what we have experienced and how others have hurt us. He wants to heal us so He can show us what a loving parent looks like.

Is there a parent you need to forgive for their harshness or abuse? Or maybe you have a grown child you need to ask forgiveness from? Commit this to prayer and ask others to lift you in prayer, too.

In **Hebrews 12:7**, we see the word *endure*, again.

What are we to endure in this verse? _____

The New American Commentary on Hebrews says the first part of Hebrews 12:7 means, "It is for discipline that you endure" or "It is because of discipline that you are enduring."[11] Discipline in the sense of exercising for health or to obtain a goal helps our fortitude. We may not start off being able to walk, let alone run a mile, but as we continue to train and discipline ourselves, we maintain longer and longer distances.

It is the same way in our spiritual lives. God's loving correction, or punishment, helps us prevail in our walk with Him. With every battle or challenge that comes our way, we grow in strength to resist temptation, or stamina for the prolonged fight.

It is because of His discipline we will be victorious in our Christian life.

Hebrews 12:7-11 explains Proverbs 3:11-12. We are the children referred to in these verses. No matter what your age, God is your Father if you know and trust in Yeshua. The verses in Hebrews 12:7-11 apply to all of us.

According to **Hebrews 12:7**, how is God treating us when He punishes us?

_____

In verses 8 through 11, we have three people spoken of: God, fathers, and sons (or children). Answer these questions based on **Hebrews 12:8-11**.

If we are without discipline, what are we considered?

_____

If we have earthly fathers who disciplined us, what should we expect from God?

_____

How did our fathers correct us? How does God correct us?

_____

How can discipline seem to us? _____

What should punishment yield?

_____

How are we trained by God? _____

The training referred to in verse 11 is like that of an athlete. It is the daily workout to get in shape for a race. Discipline gets us spiritually buff for the Christian life and the "race" we are in.

Just as we use discipline to direct our children how to behave, how to speak, and how to get along, God uses instruction and chastisement to prepare us to live holy lives.

Pink Diamond - Day Three
Joy, healing, and *new life in Christ*

My children are not perfect. We have done our best to train them in the ways of God, but we have made mistakes. I wish now I had had more patience, that I had not sweat the small stuff as often as I did and would have been a better example of God's unconditional love. It is my prayer every day they will love Yeshua more and know Him better. I ask God to make up for my mistakes and any way I have let our children down. He can do it.

God redeems the areas where we fall short. *If we are teachable,* God instructs our children and us for the rest of our lives.

Hebrews 12:12 begins with the word *Therefore,* which refers to the previous verses in Hebrews 12:7-11 on discipline.

Compare **Hebrews 12:12** with **Isaiah 35:3**. What kind of person is described in Hebrews 12:12?

_____

No Longer Lame

Going back to the racing metaphor, why does **Hebrews 12:13** tell us to make straight or level paths for our feet?

_____

_____

Read these different translations of those verses:

Common English Bible: 12 So strengthen your drooping hands and weak knees! 13 Make straight paths for your feet so that if any part is lame, it will be healed rather than injured more seriously.

New Living Translation: 12 So take a new grip with your tired hands and strengthen your weak knees. 13 Mark out a straight path for your feet so that those who are weak and lame will not fall but become strong.

New Revised Standard: 12 Therefore lift your drooping hands and strengthen your weak knees, 13 and make straight paths for your feet, so that what is lame may not be put out of joint, but rather be healed.

Lame means "crippled or physically disabled, especially in the foot or leg so as to limp or walk with difficulty."[12] These verses tell us to remove the stumbling blocks or obstacles on our path that can impede this race we are in.

What are the stumbling blocks making you lame? What obstructs your path, keeping you from setting your eyes on Yeshua and running this race?

Yeshua wants to heal you. What is the lame or disabled part of you that needs to be healed or set free?

Lameness can come from something a loved one has spoken over you or disparaging words from a teacher, coach, or other authority figure. It can come from an injustice or trauma.

Stop now and record any revelation or prayer the Holy Spirit has placed on your heart.

_____

_____

My father had a stroke when I was six years old. Although I was young, it had a profound effect on me. I knew my life would never be the same because I had lost the daddy I knew. The one who taught me to ride a bike could now barely walk. The one who had made me doughnuts at work could not feed himself. I was in constant fear of losing him completely. The fear crippled me, as the stroke had my father. I repressed the memories I could not deal with. It took ten years before I realized I needed the Lord to heal me, and about fifteen more until I no longer feared death.

That frightened, crippled little girl was an obstacle to my spiritual growth as an adult. She needed to grow up because I needed to be free.

How to Remove the Stumbling Blocks

In **Hebrews 12:14-17**, the author tells us how to make *the straight paths* from verse 13. He also tells us what we are to strive for and avoid in this Christian life. This is part of the purifying process.

Name two things we are to strive for in verse 14.

How do **Romans 12:17-18** and **2 Corinthians 13:11** clarify how we live in peace?

We studied holiness in the early chapters of Hebrews. However, what does this verse add to the fact we are to strive for holiness?

Does the gravity of this verse make you think about your life? As we have already discussed, God is serious about our holiness.

1 Thessalonians 4:7-8 (NIV) says, *For God did not call us to be impure, but to live a holy life. Therefore, anyone who rejects this instruction does not reject a human being but God, the very God who gives you his Holy Spirit.*

Hebrews 12:15 starts with the words *See to it…* or *Make sure…* There is a clear directive we are to look out for others (within the church) in two ways.

What are those two ways?

The word *fail* used in this verse means "to be left behind in the race and so fail to reach the goal, to fall short of the end."[13] We are to help others reach the goal of God's grace. I believe there is so much judgement and criticism associated with the church that the world does not see or experience grace. Too often, we kick people while they are down, instead of lifting them up.

I remember being told the reason my father had health issues was because of God's judgement on him. His sin of marrying my mom without the consent of her parents caused his stroke and heart issues. Unfortunately, many see God this way. But that is not how God works.

I am a firm believer in sowing and reaping. We reap what we sow, good or bad. If I have sex before I am married and get pregnant, I reap consequences of that decision. The baby is not a punishment. It is an outcome of the sex and intimacy between a man and woman.

I believe our food choices affect our health. Again, sowing and reaping. It is said, "We are what we eat." Bad food can cause poor health. But to think God strikes anyone with cancer, strokes, heart attacks, or dementia because of their sin is wrong.

Our punishment for rejecting God is everlasting punishment in the lake of fire. That is the final judgement. Only one righteous Person earned the right to judge because of His suffering and death, and we are not Him. We are to help people see God's grace so they can be born again into life with Christ. He does not condemn you or me. He seeks to change us from the inside out.

In **Hebrews 12:15**, what will bitterness cause? _____

How will bitterness affect others? _____

The word *defile* means to pollute or stain.[14] Bitterness does not impact one person. It pollutes the atmosphere of the church or a family. Many situations can cause this kind of resentment. Unnecessary judgement is one reason people become hostile toward the Church.

My daughter has loved the Jonas Brothers since she was twelve. They are not young boys anymore but grown men with families. I recently watched their documentary and found it sad. Their father was a pastor, so they grew up in church singing and playing music while living in the parsonage. Their church seemed to love them. But, once a non-Christian record label signed them, the church fired their father, and the family had to leave the only home they knew.

Their career did not take off immediately, and the Jonases suffered financially. A friend rented this family of six a tiny house to live in. The documentary didn't say much about the faith of their parents, but the effect of this on the three brothers was clear. It was a hurtful time for the family, and there is still resentment toward the church.

We are all responsible for our emotions and what we do with them. I am not condemning that church, because there are two sides to every story. The brothers told this story from their perspective. I have no way of knowing all the details. However, the pain they felt caused bitterness to spring up within them. I don't believe they ever went back to any church, and I can't help but wonder if that church could have handled it differently.

Pink Diamond - Day Four
Joy, healing, and *new life in Christ*

Has a church family hurt you? Years after I left a church, I remember asking the Lord if there was anyone I needed to forgive. Immediately, a dozen faces popped up in my mind. These people were from a class I had problems with when I was the Sunday school superintendent of that particular denomination.

As I pictured each face, I forgave them and asked God to bless each family. The very next week I ran into a woman from that group. I had a nice conversation with her without hurt or resentment rising within me.

If you hold bitterness or resentment toward someone you know for any reason, take the time now to forgive and ask God to bless them. It doesn't mean you condone what they did, but you are letting it go. Give it to God and ask the Lord to remove any root of bitterness within you. This is part of the purifying process to help us live in peace and holiness.

_____
_____
_____

Hebrews 12:16 is a continuation of verse 15, which begins with *See to it…* It contains the fifth and sixth instructions for making your paths straight (or getting rid of stumbling blocks).

What are the two conditions mentioned in this verse?
_____

What do the verses in **Ephesians 5:33** and **1 Corinthians 6:9** say about sexual immorality?
_____
_____

The word for godless or unholy in verse 16 also means *worldly* or *profane*.[15]

What did Esau do in verse 16?
_____

Why do you think it was considered unholy or worldly?
_____
_____

You can read more of Esau's story in **Genesis 25:29-34**. This passage says Esau despised his birthright. The word for *despised* means "to show contempt for or be of little value."[16] His birthright was the rights of the firstborn. It was an important place in the birth order of a Hebrew family. In some cases, they received a double portion of the inheritance.[17]

Esau wanted food, or we could say the desire of his flesh, more than the firstborn rights of his family. Sexual immorality is also a worldly or fleshly desire many crave satisfaction for. When the godless passions of our bodies take over, we can find ourselves wanting it more than our position in God's family.

A modern-day example of Esau's story could look like this:

A single woman who knows she needed God but doesn't want to give up relationships with different men. She wants to enjoy her different partners rather than give in to God's desire for her. She is willing to give up her birthright as a child of God for the pleasure of her flesh.

In **Hebrews 12:17**, what happen when Esau desired his inheritance back?

_____

One day we will stand before His throne and no matter how sincere, nothing will change the decision to reject Yeshua people made while on this earth. But thank God, He does not reject us while we still have breath in our lungs.

A Better Word

Before we read Hebrews 12:18-24, please turn to **Exodus 19:9-25**. This passage sets up the next portion of Hebrews. While Moses was on Mount Sinai with the Lord, the rest of Israel camped around the mountain. God wanted Moses to tell His people they were His *treasured possession* and *a kingdom of priests and a holy nation* (Ex. 19:2-6). In verse 9, we read how God came down in a cloud to talk to Moses so Israel would believe Him forever. It had been fifty days since the Passover feast, so this would be the first Pentecost. Notice in verse 16 the fire and smoke surrounding the mountain where God was.

Moses warned the people not come near the mountain, and they could not come near the Lord. This was a holy place where God was making a covenant with His people through Moses.

We read in chapter 20 the Ten Commandments as God gave them.

Read **Exodus 20:18-21**.

How did the people react to the thunder, lightning, smoke, and trumpet sound?

_____

What did Moses tell them God was doing? _____

Why? _____

Now, go back to **Hebrews 12:18-21**.

What are the first five words of verse 18? _____

List some of the things we do not come to anymore in verses 18-21.

_____

_____

_____

What is the main feeling or emotion in this passage?

_____

What are the first few words of verse 22? _____

List all the things we have come to in verse 22-24.

_____

_____

_____

What is the difference between the two portions of scripture?

_____

As we read in Exodus 20:18-21, God used His awesome power to evoke fear in Israel to keep them from sinning against Him. He wanted them to see His supremacy and authority to bring about a holy fear of Him. We no longer have that through Yeshua. We have a new covenant. A heavenly, glorious home and city where we will gather with the angels, God Himself, those who have gone before us, and Yeshua.

How is Yeshua described in verse 24?

_____

What is the last thing mentioned (that we have come to) in verse 24? What does this verse say about it? _____

Go to **Genesis 4:8-10**. What do you think Abel's blood said to God?

_____

What did Abel's blood bring? What did Yeshua's blood bring?

_____

In **Hebrews 12:24**, we see the word *better*. The blood of Yeshua is superior to any man's blood. Abel's blood spoke, and Yeshua's speaks, so ours must speak as well. That is why blood is so important to God. Murder, the spilling of innocent blood, is a horrible thing to God, whether it is from an adult or baby, born or not. I can't imagine what the blood of millions of aborted babies must cry out to God.

In **Hebrews 12:25**, we see the fifth and final warning of this book. The first sentence of this verse says, *See that you do not refuse him who is speaking*.

Who is speaking? _____

Who is "they," "we," and, "him" in verse 25?

_____

Why do you think the author warns us against refusing the One speaking?

_____

_____

Have you ever been in a situation where you didn't listen to the Holy Spirit's warning? Explain what happened.

_____

_____

_____

The Holy Spirit may warn us about a spiritual condition to correct, teach, or save us. Other times, it may be about physical protection.

Pink Diamond - Day Five
Joy, healing, and *new life in Christ*

I was at a stoplight in the left turn lane near my house. I felt a strong impression not to go on green. While I was wondering why I shouldn't, the thought came to me that the car on my right, who was in the straight lane, was going to turn left, instead. I stayed put when the light changed, and that car to my right turned in front of me to go left. I was so glad I heeded the warning of the Holy Spirit. Sometimes the Holy Spirit's warning may save you or someone else.

Hebrews 12:25 refers to the Exodus 19 and 20 passages we read earlier and to Hebrews 12:18-20.

In **Hebrews 12:25**, what didn't "they" escape?

_____

Which warning do you think would have the greater impact, the warning from earth or the warning from heaven? Why?

_____

Can you imagine standing near a mountain surrounded with smoke, fire, thunder, the sound of trumpets, and the voice of God talking to you? How frightened would you be? That was how the old covenant worked. Thank the Lord, God speaks to us through His Holy Spirit in the quietness and privacy of our hearts. That is part of the new covenant. It does not make His commands any less important or less life-changing. There were and are consequences for not listening to or denying God's voice. The Holy Spirit is real, and He is God. Regrettably, there are many churches who deny the ability of the Holy Spirit to speak to us.

Read **Hebrews 12:26-27**. The phrase, *At that time,* refers back to the time of Moses in Exodus 19 and 20.

What did God's voice do? _____

The rest of verse 26 is partially quoted in **Haggai 2:6**.

Turn to **Haggai 2:5-8**, what are the promises in verses 5 through 7?

_____

_____

Name everything God intends to shake in **Haggai 2:6-7**.

_____

The writer of Hebrews stops with the shaking of the earth and heaven. In verse 27 he explains the phrase, *Yet once more.*

What does that phrase mean according to verse 27?

_____

_____

What cannot be shaken? What do you think will remain?

_____

_____

Take a look at a similar passage of scripture in **2 Peter 3:10**. The last word of this verse is *katakaiō*, which means "to burn down (to the ground), i.e., consume wholly: —burn (up, utterly)."[18]

Everything we know, even the elements or atoms of this earth will be destroyed or removed. The heavens mentioned in Hebrews 12:26 and 2 Peter 3:10 refer to the solar systems and galaxies. Maybe this is why there will be no sun once the New Heavens and Earth are made (Rev. 22:5).

Hebrews 12:28 tells us what will not be shaken. What is it, and how should we feel about it?

_____

According to **Hebrews 12:28**, what should we give to God, and how should we offer it?

_____

_____

Finally, in verse 29, how is God described?

_____

How does that make you feel, or what does it conjure up in your mind?

_____

_____

The word *consuming* means "to destroy completely."[19] The intense pressure and heat by seismic activity can cause a diamond's molecular structure to be changed, even destroyed so that it becomes a pink color. It also frees the diamond from the impurities within it.

Most metals are purified by fire. They are heated over and over until all impurities have come to the surface to be skimmed off.

God does not want us to be impure. He may shake us up or heat things up to free us from the impurities that bind us. He wants us to be pure and holy.

What did the Lord reveal to you about yourself in this chapter?

_____

_____

How is God shaking and purifying you like the pink diamond?

_____

_____

I hope you see the discipline of the Lord as a good thing. Be teachable. Yeshua has so much to teach us.

Chapter 13 - Red Garnet
Blood, salvation, redemption, and *sacrifice*

Day One

The Antique Pyrope Hair Comb, a tiara-style hair comb from the Victorian era, is covered in beautiful, deep red, pyrope garnets.[1] These rose-cut pyrope garnets, which are the color of pomegranate seeds, are the reddest Bohemian garnets. Coming from the Greek word *pyropos*, pyrope means *fire-eyed* or *fire-like*. This beautiful hair comb was donated to the Smithsonian in 1937.[2]

The Bible refers to red garnets as carbuncles. Jewish tradition says Noah brought a carbuncle on the ark with him as a source of light. Since the sun and moon did not shine during the flood, this stone shone more brightly at night than day, helping him distinguish between the two.[3]

The red hue of this stone symbolizes *blood, salvation, redemption,* and *sacrifice*.[4] It shouldn't take long to find it.

I want to start in a rather strange place in this chapter, the end.

The author gives a little more information about this himself and this book at the end of chapter 13. Turn with me to **Hebrews 13:22-25**.

First, he asked his audience to *bear with his words of exhortation*. The Greek word for *bear* means "to accept, as valid or true."[5] I can imagine in his heart he desperately wants them to believe every word he has written about the Messiah: Yeshua is our great High Priest, who loves us and stands in intercession for us. He is the same yesterday, today, and forever. Yeshua is greater than Moses, angels, and mankind. He is the author and finisher of our faith.

God has given us this letter for the same reasons. He wants us to know His Son and believe everything written about Him in Scripture. God wants us to know how much we are *loved*.

What can we conclude about Timothy from verse 23?

_____

This author knows Timothy and wants to travel with him to see the people to whom he wrote the letter. I, personally, do not believe the author of Hebrews is Paul. In every letter written by Paul, he introduces himself and his co-authors within the first line. Why wouldn't he do that in this letter?

From what I have learned, Hebrews' author used both the literary and elaborate Greek of a highly educated man. It was unlike the Greek used to translate documents from Hebrew. At least 150 of his words are unlike the vocabulary of the rest of the New Testament books, and Hebrews' structure is more like the Greek rhetoric style used in speeches of persuasion.[6] We do not know who wrote it, only the type of person who did.

In verse 24, there is the exchange of greetings. The author sends a greeting from *those who come from Italy*. This may mean the author is in Italy while writing this letter or is with Italian people as he writes. We know little, since this is all the author has given us.

Hebrews 13 seems to be a list of commands for the body of believers to abide by. It was as if the author had so much more to say but needed to end this letter, which is why he writes, "I have written to you briefly," in verse 22.

We will consider each command, starting in **Hebrews 13:1-5**.

In Hebrews 12:28, the author encourages us to be grateful for an unshakable kingdom by offering worship and service to God with reference and awe.

How does Hebrews 13:1-2 suggest we do that?

_____

We are all to love our brothers and sisters in Christ, but do you know someone who exemplifies that? A person who, no matter what, is able to encourage, love, and take care of others? Who?

_____

We are to love those inside and outside the church. Is one easier for you than the other?

_____

We can have higher expectations of those we worship with than those we work or socialize with. It was a surprise when someone in my church was rude to me or cursed in conversation. We are each at different places in our maturity with the Lord. All Bible-believing churches should have non-believers attending. It's where they belong, right?

There is a difference between saying we are Christians and letting Yeshua be LORD over our hearts, minds, and souls. This is a major reason there can be a variance between people within the same church. Does Yeshua have a say in what you watch, listen to, and do each day?

Are you a Christian trying to walk the walk in your strength or a Christian who has surrendered everything to Yeshua, letting Him direct your life? Explain why or why not.

_____

_____

_____

Red Garnet - Day Two
Blood, salvation, redemption, and *sacrifice*

I love to have people over to my house. Being an extrovert, I find a great deal of pleasure being with those I love, if only to sit and visit for an hour. My mother always had people over to our small house. Just about every Sunday we had company, whether it was my aunts, uncles, and cousins, or our church family. For many of my kids' younger years, I did the same thing. Even now when my kids see me really cleaning, they ask, "Who's coming over?" Making people feel welcome in your home, no matter how it looks, is true hospitality.

In **Hebrews 13:2**, the author tells us by showing hospitality to strangers, we may be entertaining angels. Notice he does not say, *If there are angels…* but suggests there are angels among us.

Have you ever had an encounter with an angel? If so, what was it like?

_____

_____

_____

It can be hard to believe in the supernatural. But we live at the junction of the natural (world) and supernatural, or spiritual, realms. I believe we don't experience more of the spiritual realm (angels and Holy Spirit) because of our unbelief. That is just where Satan wants us, too.

Many people who live in third world countries *know* there is a spiritual world (not just of the angelic kind) because they have experienced it firsthand by the sorcery and witchcraft taking place around them. It is not surprising to people like this to see the power of the Holy Spirit and believe.

I know a couple who lives in the States, but they were born and raised in a Muslim country. Yeshua's appearance transformed them as they listened to Him tell of His love for them. He rocked their world. Supernatural protection and amazing answers to prayer happened daily as they sought to leave their country to come where they were free to worship Yeshua.

Ask someone who has worshipped Satan and had the love of Christ change them. They will tell you how real the spiritual realm is. God does powerful deliverances in these men and women as He turns their lives around and they experience the joy and power of the Holy Spirit.

The most common command in the Bible is to "remember." After giving Noah a rainbow, God said He would remember His covenant to Noah and every living thing (Gen. 9:15). Each feast is a remembrance of what God did for the Israelites. We are to remember the Sabbath and keep it holy (Ex. 20:8). We are to remember Yeshua's death by partaking in Communion. How many can you think of?

Who are we told to remember in **Hebrews 13:3**? How are we to remember them?

_____

_____

In this passage, *those in prison* and *those who are mistreated (suffering)* specifically refer to Christians. Although, the same could be said of anyone who is imprisoned, suffering, or mistreated, not just those in the Church.

As you know, most scholars believe the Messianic Jews of this book were persecuted for believing in the Messiah.

How does this verse speak to you concerning those imprisoned and mistreated for Christ throughout the world?

_____

_____

Read **Hebrews 13:4**. Marriage can be a hot topic and a sensitive one. It would be great if we, as Christians, were all perfect and always got along with each other, including our spouses. However, that's not reality. I am writing this as a person who has never been divorced, so I want to be respectful and sensitive to those who have been.

There are different reasons people have divorced, and this study is not to condemn or condone divorce but say what the Bible says about it. If your marriage has fallen apart or is about to, *God knows your pain*. He has compassion for you. Our job as the Church is not to kick you when you are down, but to lift each other in prayer and treat one another with love and understanding; guiding each other toward forgiveness and healing.

Believe it or not, this is not an issue of just our generation. During the time of Yeshua, there were two types of teachings on marriage. The two schools of thought were from the School of Hillel and the School of Shammai. Hillel and Shammai were Pharisees.

Read **Matthew 19:3**. The Pharisees asked Yeshua about the lawfulness of divorcing a wife for any reason because of a popular teaching by Hillel. According to him, a man could divorce his wife for ruining his food.[7] Shammai believed a man could only divorce because of his wife's unfaithfulness.[8]

Yeshua tells them everything we need to know by answering this question.

1. God made us male and female.
2. A man should leave his mother and father.
3. The man and his wife become one flesh.
4. What God joins no one should separate.
5. Moses allowed divorce, not God.

Yeshua also said, *"Whoever divorces his wife, except for sexual immorality, and marries another, commits adultery."* This is a verse that gets taken out of context a lot. Is this verse saying if you marry another after being divorce you are committing adultery? Brad H. Young, Ph.D., Hebrew University, says, "No." In his book, *Jesus, the Jewish Theologian*, he suggested the clearer meaning of this verse in Hebrew would be, "Everyone who divorces his wife [in order] to marry another commits adultery."[9] If I divorced my husband because I want to marry another man, that is the same as adultery in God's eyes. If two people were to divorce for any reason, and one re-marries later, that person is not committing adultery.

Does God hate divorce? Yes (Mal. 2:14-16, NLT). Does God hate abuse and adultery? Yes. The best thing anyone can do in a bad marriage is to seek God. Let Him direct you. Seek godly counsel and be in the Word. The Holy Spirit will direct you. Last, pray for your spouse, no matter what they have done or how you feel about them. Give them to the Lord.

Red Garnet - Day Three
Blood, salvation, redemption, and *sacrifice*

What does it mean for the marriage bed to be undefiled? Hebrews 7:26 also uses the word undefiled. It means "pure, or untainted."[10] Sex is to be only between a man and his wife. God judges the *unrepentant* sexually immoral person and the adulterer.

How would you describe repentance? How might it look?

_____

_____

Repentance is more than confessing our sin. It includes turning from it and walking in the opposite way.

Read **Hebrews 13:5-6**. How do these two verses relate to each other?

_____

_____

What are we to keep free from?

_____

Turn to **Matthew 6:22-24**. Verses 22 and 23 are a Hebrew idiom. The healthy eye represents generosity, while the bad eye symbolizes selfishness.

According to verse 23, if your eye is bad, what will be the condition of your body?

_____

So, what does it mean when the verse says, *The eye is a lamp of the body?*

_____

This idiom is why verse 24 tells us, *You cannot serve God and money [possessions].*

Read **Hebrews 13:7-9**. What directive does the author give us in verse 7?

_____

Which leaders should be remembered?

_____

Skip verse 8 for now and read verse 9. Apparently, there was false teaching going around concerning the value of sacrificed animals as food. It is believed by some scholars this meant by eating the meat, which was sacrificed, there would be greater grace for the one who ate it. There are many opinions about the meaning of verses 9 through 11.

However, this verse seems to correlate to **Colossians 2:16**. Because of the dietary laws given in the Torah, many Messianic Jews were targeted with false teachings. Sometimes it is still confusing to us Gentiles.

What does this author warn us in verse 9?

_____

In verse 7, we are told to remember our leaders and the outcome of their life and faith, and in verse 9 we are warned not to be led away by diverse and strange teachings. Verse 8 says, *Jesus Christ is the same yesterday and today and forever.*

Why do you think verse 8 is nestled in between verses 7 and 9?

_____

_____

Please read **Hebrews 13:10-12**. In verse 10, the author refers to an altar from which no one may eat.

This altar is mentioned in **Exodus 25:10-22**. What is this altar? What was it used for?

_____

According to **Hebrews 13:11**, why couldn't the priests eat of this sacrificed meat?

_____

In this scripture passage, the author is referring to Yom Kippur. **Leviticus 16** explains the process of sacrifice God expected during Yom Kippur. Read it over but pay attention to verses 23 through 28.

Once the sacrifice was made by the priest, what happened to the animals' bodies? Where did this happen?

_____

Hebrews 13:12 tells us where our Lamb was sacrificed. **Luke 23:32-33** tells us the name of this place.

What is the name of the place where Yeshua was crucified? _____

Red Garnet - Day Four
Blood, salvation, redemption, and *sacrifice*

During the time of Yeshua, Golgotha was outside the walls of Jerusalem. Today, there is a church in this place called the Church of the Holy Sepulchre. Within this church, there is a chapel called the *Chapel of Adam*.[11] It is the place where Adam's skull is buried. According to Aaron Eime,[12] Bible Historian and Deacon of Christ Church in Jerusalem, tradition holds that God created Adam in this area (the Garden of Eden was in Jerusalem) and he was buried below Golgotha. The first Adam was born and buried here, and the last Adam (Yeshua, 1 Cor. 15:45-47) died above his grave. (I know this may not be the popular belief for the location for the Garden of Eden, but Rev. Aaron Eime makes a compelling argument for it.)

Aaron teaches the Jewish tradition claims Creation began in Jerusalem. If this is true, it is also the place where sin and death entered our world and the place where our Savior conquered sin and death. God does not work on a linear timeline but a circular one. Jewish tradition says, "beginnings and ends always end in the same place."[13]

Why did Yeshua suffer outside the gate?

_____

It was to make us holy so we can have a relationship with the Father. Are you becoming holy or staying the same—comfortable?

Read **Hebrews 13:13-14**.

In verse 13, where does the author tell us to go? Why?

_____

What does this mean to you?

_____

_____

The Greek word for reproach is *oneidismos*, and it means "insult, disgrace, implying public reproach."[14]

I believe the author is telling his audience to leave the camp they knew, Judaism, and follow Yeshua. But, in doing so, they will endure the same disgrace and/or persecution Yeshua did. I believe we can relate the same idea to ourselves.

Are we willing to walk away from the familiar to follow Yeshua and bear the same insults and disgrace our Savior bore, even to the point of death? Take your time answering this question. It's a serious one.

Kayla Mueller was an American humanitarian worker in Syria. ISIS kidnapped and held her captive for years, while she suffered repeated beatings and rape at their hands. Kayla refused to renounce her faith in Yeshua, and ISIS killed her. It is said she even stayed behind when others escaped so they would have a better chance of getting away. Her only concern was for the Syrian people she had gone there to help.[15]

Hebrews 13:14, starts with the words, *So here…* which refers to outside the camp, where our Lord is.

What do you think the author means by, *we have no lasting city...?*

_____

_____

We are all part of the kingdom of God; no matter your country, color, ethnicity, age, gender, or economic standing, if you are a child of the King and believe in the name of the Yeshua HaMashiach (Jesus the Messiah) you are a part of His Kingdom, now. Our home is not here, but we wait for the home or city that is to come.

Read **Revelation 21:9-27**. Both Heaven and Earth suffered corruption by sin. Revelation 12 tells us about a war in Heaven, where Satan battled against Michael, the archangel, until he was cast out of Heaven with a third of the angels. Since sin has entered both Heaven and Earth, they must be made new. Revelation 21 gives a beautiful description of the New Jerusalem. I believe this is the city the author is speaking of.

In **Hebrews 13:15-16**, we see two different sacrifices we are to give.

What are they?

_____

_____

In verse 15, what is the sacrifice of praise considered?

_____

Read **Isaiah 57:19** and **Hosea 14:2**. In both these verses, we see the phrase *fruit (vow) of the lips*. In Jewish tradition, prayer is the highest form of worship; specifically, prayers said aloud. Praise should be a huge part of our prayers. This is the fruit of our lips: acknowledging the name of the Lord.

Turn to **Micah 6:7-8**. Micah 6:8 is one of my favorite verses.

What is being contrasted in these verses?

_____

_____

In Isaiah 58, God spells out what it means to fast. He gives examples of the wrong way in **Isaiah 58:1-5**, and the right way in verses in **Isaiah 58:6-7**. The rest of Isaiah 58 tells of God's promises and the outpouring of His blessings when we get it right.

Record anything you can improve in your walk with the Lord from these verses.

_____

_____

This is God's kind of sacrifice. He wants us all to make these sacrifices. Ask the Lord to make us better at helping the broken, the bound, and those with serious physical needs.

Red Garnet - Day Five
Blood, salvation, redemption, and sacrifice

Years ago, I was the Sunday school superintendent of the church we attended. This meant I created classes, put teachers in place for them, and oversaw the classes. I also had a small board who helped with all this, as well as voted on various aspects of the classes. A young college graduate came to me wanting to teach a class. As he was telling me about the class, I felt the Holy Spirit "yelling," "No, no, no, no." Seriously, I could barely hear what the man was saying. I took his curriculum suggestions to the board and they voted "No."

I left this young man the answer in a voicemail. He called me back later yelling about his displeasure at this decision. I was a bit taken aback by his behavior and called my pastor. After meeting with this man, my pastor decided to let him have his class and curriculum. I was a bit disappointed to put it lightly…But I let it go because not only was he the pastor and had the final say, but he was in authority over me. Despite what the Lord had told me, I was not responsible for the pastor's decision. I was obedient.

Today, read **Hebrews 13:17-18**.

What is the command? Why does the author command this?

_____

_____

In verse 17, who is held accountable? _____

Compare verse 17 with verse 7. In a culture of independence, we can lack a healthy respect for authority in the church, school, and government. Hebrews 13:17 may prove difficult for some people. It requires discernment to know the ones we obey are living according to God's morals and laws (within the church). That is why Hebrews 13:7 says, *to consider the outcome of their way of life*. Are our church leaders living godly and holy lives? Then imitate and obey them. This is a command.

Our society does not like the word "obey," which is why many have it removed from wedding vows. If we cannot obey God-given authority on the earth, then we will have trouble obeying God's authority.

How should the leaders within the church keep watch over our souls?

_____

To do so with groaning would be no advantage (the literal Greek word in this verse) to anyone. If our leaders "watch over our souls" without the proper godly attitude, then they may as well be replaced. I believe this is why the author writes Hebrews 13:18.

Why does the author want prayer?

_____

In verse 19, where does the author want to be? _____

The author switches "us" to "I" in this verse. This could imply he has a relationship with his audience and has lived among them for a time. We do not know if this author was imprisoned or was ministering in other countries. The Greek term *restored* can also mean *sent back*.

Hebrews 13:20-21 is the benediction for the book of Hebrews. Can you believe we have studied this entire book already? I hope you learned as much as I did. I also pray you experienced Yeshua in a way you never have before.

Look how this author describes the Father and Son from verse 20. Record it here.

God - _____

Yeshua - _____

How Yeshua was raised from the dead? - _____

In verse 21, what did the author pray God would do in our lives?

_____

How does God equip us according to this verse?

_____

To perform a task or carry out the Lord's will, we need to be equipped by Him. The Greek word for *equip* means to "make adequate, furnish completely, make sufficient, and in some contexts, mend, or restore."[16]

Turn to **2 Timothy 3:16-17** and **Ephesians 4:11-16**.

How does God equip us in 2 Timothy 3:16-17?

_____

_____

How does God equip us in Ephesians 4:11-12?

_____

_____

If we think of the word *equip* in the context of *mending* or *restoring* as the definition suggests, it could imply we may need healing (emotional or spiritual) as a preparation to do His will. I believe to do God's will and His work to the best of our ability involves being made whole through Yeshua's transforming power in our heart and soul.

I pray you have both heard and obeyed the voice of the Holy Spirit throughout this study. If you have not already, I pray you may forgive those who have wounded you and find freedom from strongholds like fear, rejection, shame, and addiction. Let Yeshua mend, repair, and restore you to the person He wants you to be without the bondage that holds us captive.

In the last part of verse 21, what does the Lord want to work in us?

_____

Everything the Lord wants to do in us is pleasing in His sight. But it is natural for us to resist those very things. God is transforming us into the image of His Son. This is not an easy process for us. However, it is necessary if we want to walk in obedience and mature in our faith. Accepting Yeshua as our Lord and Savior is only the first step in our Christian life. Holiness is a lifelong process, which God will not finish until Heaven. Don't give up! Keep running the race.

Let us run with endurance the race that is set before us, looking to [Yeshua], the founder and perfecter of our faith… Hebrews 12:1-2.

Please record any final thoughts or comments.

_____

_____

_____

I pray this study has been a blessing to you and God has done a deep work within you. I have enjoyed this expedition through Hebrews with you. I have pictured your faces, imagined your needs, and felt the hurt this life has thrown at you as I have written this study. Thank you for letting me join you on this journey to freedom and a deeper life in Christ.

In the words of Hebrews' author, *Grace be with all of you* (Heb. 13:25).

I love you all!

The Jewels of Hebrews
Leader's Guide

The Jewels of Hebrews is for an individual or a small group study. It is a thirteen-week Bible study with each week divided into five daily lessons that include a mix of teaching, scripture reading, reflection, and question and answer fill-in. JOH can be done in twelve weeks if the group begins Chapter 1 before the first day of class.

Each chapter is named for a different gemstone whose color describes an attribute of our Savior as revealed in the book of Hebrews. In this verse-by-verse study, the student will discover the meaning of the jewel's color as it applies to Yeshua, as well as uncovering wounds, unforgiveness, and strongholds preventing the fullness of their walk with Him. If they are willing, each person will hear from the Holy Spirit, grow closer to their Savior, and know His love for them as they experience healing.

For small groups, it is important for the facilitator to ask questions and promote discussion within the group by asking both biblical and reflective questions. Below is a guide to use with each chapter.

Chapter 1 – Amethyst
Start off each chapter by answering any questions over the material done for that week.

Day 1: a. What strikes you most about the first four verses?
b. How does the Holy Spirit speak to you?
Day 2: a. What does Ps. 2:8 and Daniel 7:13-14 state about Yeshua's inheritance? How is His kingdom and dominion described?
b. How does understanding the pictorial name for Elohim affect the way you see the Father, Son, and Holy Spirit?
Day 3: a. Considering points 3 and 4, the author suggests Yeshua can be found in the Old Testament, especially in Exodus 24:9-11. What are your thoughts?
b. What characteristics of God in Psalm 145 do you need today?
Day 4: a. Have you considered your relationship with God a friendship and sonship? How does this knowledge make you see God differently?
b. What type of healing do you need? (Pray for those needs).
Day 5: a. Why does the author spend so much time trying to convince us Yeshua is greater than the angels?
b. Where is the amethyst in this chapter? Which verses did you uncover regarding royalty, majesty, and kingship?

Chapter 2 – Topaz
Start off each chapter by answering any questions over the material done for that week.

Day 1: a. Please read **Hebrews 2:1-4**. In the first verse, we read the first of five exhortations or appeals. What is the first appeal? What is the outcome if we don't do what the writer is admonishing us to do?
b. Was there anyone you needed to forgive this week? Is there anyone willing to share?
Day 2: a. Discuss legalism and its effects on the church.
b. Ask for a volunteer to discuss their freedom from fear.
Day 3: a. How do you see Yeshua (Jesus)?

b. Discuss this question: Ask Yeshua to show His feelings for you. Write what He shows you.

Day 4: a. Have you ever thought about the meaning of glory? How would you describe "glory" to someone else?

b. What ways has God used to perfect you?

Day 5: a. Are you experiencing freedom? Why? Why not?

b. Please record anything the Lord showed or spoke to you from this chapter. Did He reveal anything new about Himself or who you are to Him?

Chapter 3 – Emerald
Start off each chapter by answering any questions over the material done for that week.

Day 1: a. Is God Jehovah to you? Is He everything, and everything you will ever need?

b. Do you consider yourself a friend of God? Why or why not?

Day 2: a. Read **John 6:41-43** again and compare it with **Exodus 16:6-12**. What are the people doing? Why? Do you ever find yourself like the people in Exodus?

b. How is the Great Commission being fulfilled today? How do you think you are fulfilling the Great Commission?

Day 3: a. Who or what has built you? Can you name a few people or events?

b. Ask Him to reveal how He designed you from your conception. Ask for a volunteer to share.

Day 4: a. What is the main reason a whole generation of people died in the wilderness instead of entering the Promised Land?

b. Is anyone willing to share how you dealt with unbelief in your Christian walk?

Day 5: a. Why do you think rebellion was dealt with in such severity in the Old Testament?

b. What verses led you to the beautiful green of the emerald?

Chapter 4 – Onyx
Start off each chapter by answering any questions over the material done for that week.

Day 1: a. How can you turn what you *understand* (intellectually) about Yeshua into what your heart *knows* (believes) about Yeshua?

Day 2: a. What rest do you think the author is referring to in **Hebrews 4:1**? Why?

b. Look at **Exodus 23:20-22**. Have you ever read something similar? Whom does this angel sound like? What does God warn them against?

Day 3: a. Rest. What does it mean to you?

b. According to this verse, why did God command His people to keep the Sabbath?

Day 4: a. Please read **Hebrews 4:10-11**. For what are we to strive?

b. What verses or names did you include that have the word living, life, or alive?

Day 5: a. What are practical ways we can avoid being unbalanced in the Spirit or the Word?

b. Is there anything the Holy Spirit revealed to you in this chapter regarding rest or God's Word?

Chapter 5 – Sapphire
Start off each chapter by answering any questions over the material done for that week.

Day 1: a. What happens when we approach God's throne with boldness?

b. What area do you need wisdom?

Day 2: a. Please turn to and read **Matthew 25:31-46** and **2 Corinthians 5:10-11**. What do these verses reveal to us about Yeshua?

b. What can our conduct as Christians in public reveal to others?

Day 3: a. If we call Him Father, how are we to conduct ourselves?

b. Discussion: *If the world accepts you, chances are you will not be acceptable to God.*

Day 4: a. According to **Hebrews 5:8-9**, what did Yeshua learn through His suffering? What made Yeshua perfect?

b. In the Hebrew and Greek languages, the act of hearing means obeying. This is not how our culture understands "hearing." Discuss this.

Day 5: a. What results when we live on milk?

b. Are there any ways you feel the Lord wants to train you in righteousness?

Chapter 6 – Opal
Start off each chapter by answering any questions over the material done for that week.

Day 1: a. What does the author consider the "elementary doctrine of Christ"?

b. If suffering perfected Yeshua, what do you think it does for us? Explain.

Day 2: a. What will we do if God permits?

b. According to Hebrews 6:6, what is being done to the Son of God? How can we do that?

Day 3: a. What does deny yourself mean, and how would you explain this to someone?

b. Discuss this statement: God's nature will not allow Him to be anything but fair and righteous. Do you believe it?

Day 4: a. Are there any promises you are waiting on God to fulfill?

b. In the six different scriptures in which you read the promises of God, did any stand out to you? Which one and why?

Day 5: a. What did God show to the "heirs of the promise"?

b. Where was the opal in this chapter? Where did you find promises of God?

Chapter 7 – Hope Diamond
Start off each chapter by answering any questions over the material done for that week.

Day 1: a. What loss have you experienced and how did God comfort you?

Day 2: a. What does tithing mean to you?

b. Discuss this statement in regard to the tithe: "*The emphasis of the perfect is not the past action so much as it is as such but the present 'state of affairs' resulting from the past action.*" This definition is saying the perfect tense describes something that happened in the past, but because of the action, it continues into the present.

Day 3: a. Why wasn't perfection attainable through the Levitical priesthood?

b. What "can't" statements do you want to share?

Day 4: a. What *better hope* was introduced?

b. Since Yeshua's priesthood is permanent and continues forever, what can He do that the Levitical priest could not? What does this mean to you?

Day 5: a. God doesn't just say, "Seek Me." How does He want us to seek Him?

b. What are the characteristics of our High Priest? Discuss some of the answers to the comparison exercise.

Chapter 8 – Pearl
Start off each chapter by answering any questions over the material done for that week.

Day 1: a. How did the author refer to God in verse 1? How is our High Priest described in these two verses?

b. How does the author describe the true Tent or Tabernacle in Hebrews 8:2?

Day 2: a. How do you approach God in prayer? Discuss the parts of the tabernacle mentioned and how they relate to how we can approach God.

Day 3: a. Discuss the meaning of the letters and their names within the Hebrew word for tabernacle, *mischan*, spelled משכן.

b. In **Leviticus 17:10-11**, what does the blood do for the people? How does it do it?

Day 4: a. Ask who has been to a Seder or Passover meal. Discuss what they learned.

Day 5: a. Hebrews 8:9 tells us this covenant will not be like the old Mosaic covenant. Why?

b. According to **Matthew 13:52**, the Lord is training us for the Kingdom of Heaven. In what ways do you feel He is training you?

Chapter 9 – Ruby
Start off each chapter by answering any questions over the material done for that week.

Day 1: a. What does worship mean to you?

b. How do we worship in truth and Spirit?

Day 2: a. How does **Isaiah 53:2** and **Hebrews 7:26,** help us understand how Yeshua is like the acacia wood?

b. Have you ever been in a similar situation? Has God ever kept you from something and you blamed it on someone else? Or has God said "no" to you only to realize later He protected you?

Day 3: a. According to **Numbers 18:1,** how did God explain the priest's duty concerning the sanctuary and priesthood?

b. Have you ever considered how you might have responded if you were in Jerusalem at the time of Yeshua's crucifixion? Would you have screamed, "Crucify Him!" or begged for Him to be saved?

Day 4: a. What was purified with the blood of goats and bulls? What was purified with the blood of Christ?

b. What do the people say in response to the reading of the Book of the Covenant? How would you answer Moses' question from Exodus 24:1-8?

Day 5: a. Discuss: Do you see how Yeshua was able "to put away sin" once for all? His blood covers our sin and changes how God sees us. Because of this, we "appear" clean to God, who sees Yeshua's blood instead of our sin. This is why we can approach Him and His throne to be in His presence. Yeshua is the priest who entered *the* Holy Place and sacrificed Himself. Does this change how you approach God? Why?

b. If there was a verse or "ruby" that spoke to you in this chapter, please share it.

Chapter 10 – Golden Diamond
Start off each chapter by answering any questions over the material done for that week.

Day 1: a. What Old Testament Scriptures do Hebrews 10:5-7 come from? Who wrote those OT verses?

b. Discuss: Obedience is how we show our love to God. He does not want us to work our fingers to the bone for Him unless He calls us to do it. If He calls us to rest, then we should be obedient to what He says. All the sacrifices we make of our time and efforts (busyness), or all the money and offerings we give in His name will not please God as much as our obedience to Him.

Day 2: a. In my Bible, a number one is after Christ in verse twelve. It signifies the Greek manuscripts said this one instead of Christ. Why do you think the original Greek said this one instead of Christ?

b. Why do you think the author quoted parts of Psalm 110:1 in Hebrews so much?

Day 3: a. Go over **Hebrews 10:19-25** and the two *since* or *having* phrases along with the three *Let us* phrases.

b. Discuss: Please think about the *Let us* phrases. Which of these might you consider difficult?

Can you draw near to God in faith? Is your hope wavering? Or do you doubt God's promises or faithfulness? Do you find it difficult to stir others up to love and produce good works?

Day 4: a. Describe a time in your life when you needed your church. What was happening in your life at the time and how did the church's response make you feel?

b. The author gives three characteristics of a person who deserves punishment in verse 29. What are they?

Day 5: a. In Hebrews 10:30-31, what is God's reaction to apostasy in these verses?

b. What spoke to you in Hebrews 10? What nuggets of gold did God show you about your faith?

Chapter 11 – Lapis Luzuli
Start off each chapter by answering any questions over the material done for that week.

Day 1: a. Read **Hebrews 11:1,** and in your own words record the meaning of faith.

b. Discuss: Faith is what sets us apart from everyone else.

Day 2: a. Here are a few more verses that speak of drawing near to God. Record how each of these verses wants us to approach God. Discuss the answers to each of these scripture verses: Hebrews 10:22, James 4:8, Psalm 145:18.

b. Is God telling you to build an "ark"? What is it? How are others responding to your "ark"?

Day 3: a. In your own words, what was Abram expecting from God?

b. What aspirations have you been dreaming of but feel too old to achieve or do?

Day 4: a. Are you focused on the world you live in today or the one to come? What are ways we can help change the future for our descendants?

b. How do you "see" God in your life? How and when has He shown up?

Day 5: a. Discuss the question: So why are we surprised when people reject, mock or desert us because of our faith?

b. In *My Utmost for His Highest*, Oswald Chambers wrote, "Faith must be tested, because it can be turned into a personal possession only through conflict. What is your faith up against right now?" How would you answer his question?

Chapter 12 – Pink Diamond
Start off each chapter by answering any questions over the material done for that week.

Day 1: a. In your Christian life, which runner describes you? Why?

b. What are some ways we can keep our eyes on Yeshua while in this race?

Day 2: a. Read Ephesians 1:20, 2:4-6. Both passages are referring to God and notice they are in past tense, too. What do these verses mean to you?

b. Have you ever felt the Lord's discipline? If yes, what was it like?

Day 3: a. We studied holiness in the early chapters of Hebrews. However, what does this verse add to the fact we are to strive for holiness?

b. How will bitterness affect others?

Day 4: a. What do the verses in **Ephesians 5:33** and **1 Corinthians 6:9** say about sexual immorality?

b. Have you ever been in a situation where you didn't listen to the Holy Spirit's warning? Explain what happened.

Day 5: a. Which warning do you think would have the greater impact, the warning from earth or the warning from heaven? Why?

b. In Hebrews 12:28, how is God described? How does that make you feel or what does it conjure up in your mind?

Chapter 13 – Red Garnet

Start off each chapter by answering any questions over the material done for that week.

Day 1: a. We are to love those inside and outside the church. Is one easier for you than the other?

b. Are you a Christian trying to walk the walk in your strength or a Christian who has surrendered everything to Yeshua, letting Him direct your life? Explain why or why not.

Day 2: a. Have you ever had an encounter with an angel? If so, what was it like?

b. How does this verse speak to you concerning those imprisoned and mistreated for Christ throughout the world?

Day 3: a. How would you describe repentance? How might it look?

b. Why do you think verse 8 is nestled in between verses 7 and 9?

Day 4: a. What do you think the author means by, "we have no lasting city…"?

b. Record anything you can improve in your walk with the Lord from **Isaiah 58:6-7**.

Day 5: a. How should the leaders within the church keep watch over our souls?

b. How does God equip us according to Hebrews 13:20-21?

c. Final thoughts or comments. Anything learned that someone wants to share.

Thank you so much for your obedience to Yeshua! I pray this has blessed you and your class.

ABOUT THE AUTHOR

Stephanie Pavlantos is passionate about getting people into God's Word. She has taught Bible studies for fifteen years and has spoken at ladies' retreats.

She is published in *Refresh* Bible study magazine, *Charisma* magazine, and CBN.com. She is also a contributor for *www.Faithbeyondfear.com* and Feed Your Soul with the Word of God compilation by *Lighthousebiblestudies.com*. You can visit her blog at *www.stephaniepavlantos.com* and other social media sites at Twitter *@DPavlantos* and *www.facebook.com/stephaniepavlantos*.

Her Hebrews study won third place at Blue Ridge Mountain Christian Writers Conference and an Honorable Mention at the Florida Christian Writers Conference.

Married for twenty-eight years, she and Mike have three children: Matthew, Alexandria, and Michael. Stephanie loves animals and has dogs, ducks, goats, and chickens.

Endnotes

[1] Encyclopaedia Britannica, "Aramaic Language", 2019 Encyclopaedia Britannica, Inc. https://www.britannica.com/topic/Aramaic-language, April 22, 2019.

Chapter 1

[1] "Famous Birthstones: Amethyst – the Duchess of Windsor's Necklace", http://4cs.gia.edu/en-us/blog/famous-birthstones-duchess-windsors-amethyst-necklace/

[2] Howard Cohen of HSC Communications, 2011 https://thejewelerblog.wordpress.com/2016/02/04/amethyst-here-are-10-fun-facts-about-the-february-birthstone/

[3] Crownover, Rose, "Amethyst" Stones of the Bible 2007-2012, April 3, 2018http://www.preciousstonesofthebible.com/stonegallery.html

[4] Crownover, Rose, "Amethyst" Stones of the Bible 2007-2012, April 3, 2018http://www.preciousstonesofthebible.com/colorsymbolism.html

[5] James Swanson, Dictionary of Biblical Languages with Semantic Domains: Greek (New Testament) (Oak Harbor: Logos Research Systems, Inc., 1997).

[6] Blue Letter Bible, Clarence Larkin, Chapter 28. Types And Antitypes https://www.blueletterbible.org/study/larkin/dt/28.cfm, March, 2017

[7] https://www.merriam-webster.com/dictionary/heir

[8] Rock Island Books, C.J. Lovik, https://www.youtube.com/watch?v=X7MpzFLbWLo

[9] Strong, J. 1996. The exhaustive concordance of the Bible : Showing every word of the test of the common English version of the canonical books, and every occurrence of each word in regular order. (electronic ed.) . Woodside Bible Fellowship.: Ontario

[10] Bible Study Tools, Orr, James, M.A., D.D. General Editor. "Entry for 'SHEKINAH'". "International Standard Bible Encyclopedia". 1915. https://www.biblestudytools.com/dictionary/shekinah/ July 29, 2019.

[11] ibid

[12] Strong, J. 1996. *The exhaustive concordance of the Bible : Showing every word of the test of the common English version of the canonical books, and every occurrence of each word in regular order.* (electronic ed.) . Woodside Bible Fellowship.: Ontario

[13] http://thussaidthelord.com/as-it-is-written-2/ March 2017.

[14] Strong, J. 1996. *The exhaustive concordance of the Bible: Showing every word of the text of the common English version of the canonical books, and every occurrence of each word in regular order.* (Electronic ed.) . Woodside Bible Fellowship.: Ontario

[15] Johns Hopkins Medicine, Health, "Forgiveness: Your Health Depends on it." 2019https://www.hopkinsmedicine.org/health/wellness-and-prevention/forgiveness-your-health-depends-on-it, Aug. 4, 2019.

[16] Jewish New Testament Commentary, David H. Stern, 1992, 664.

16 Wiersbe, W. W. 1996, c1989. The Bible exposition commentary. "An exposition of the New Testament comprising the entire 'BE' series"--Jkt. Victor Books: Wheaton, Ill

Chapter 2

[1]Internet Stones.com, Braganza "Diamond", https://www.internetstones.com/braganza-diamond.html, June 5, 2018

[2] Crownover, Rose, Precious Stones of the Bible, "Topaz" Stones of the Bible 2007-2012 https://www.gemselect.com/topaz/topaz.php, April 4, 2018

3 Crownover, Rose, Precious Stones of the Bible, "Topaz" Stones of the Bible 2007-2012
http://www.preciousstonesofthebible.com/colorsymbolism.html,
4 Hobart M. King, Ph.D., RPG, Geology.com, " Mohs Hardness Scale" https://geology.com/minerals/mohs-hardness-scale.shtml
5 James Swanson, Dictionary of Biblical Languages with Semantic Domains: Greek (New Testament) (Oak Harbor: Logos Research Systems, Inc., 1997).
6 ibid
7 ibid
8 Strong, J. 1996. The exhaustive concordance of the Bible : Showing every word of the test of the common English version of the canonical books, and every occurrence of each word in regular order. (electronic ed.) . Woodside Bible Fellowship.: Ontario

Chapter 3

1 The Royal Order of Sartorial Splendor, "Readers' Top 15 Tiaras: #6. The Grand Duchess Vladimir Tiara," http://orderofsplendor.blogspot.com/2011/12/readers-top-15-tiaras-6-grand-duchess.html, Nov. 1, 2018.
2 Gemporia, Learning Library, "CLEOPATRA'S EMERALDS", https://www.gemporia.com/en-us/learning-library/terms/cleopatra%E2%80%99s%20emeralds/ Nov. 1, 2018.
3 Dunne, Carey, Fast Company, "A Glittering Visual History Of Emeralds," Jan. 22, 2014,
https://www.fastcompany.com/3025057/a-glittering-visual-history-of-emeralds
4 Crownover, Rose, Precious Stones of the Bible, "Emerald" Stones of the Bible 2007-2012, April 3, 2018http://www.preciousstonesofthebible.com/stonegallery.html
5 The Emerald Jeweler, "Clarity," Oct. 8, 2009, https://naturalemerald.wordpress.com/tag/emerald-flaws/ Nov. 1, 2018.
6 Arthur, Kay, *To Know Him by Name*, Multnomah Books, 1995. Pages 61 and 64.
7 Rock Island Books, C.J. Lovik, https://www.youtube.com/watch?time_continue=6&v=Lp_MvUIoQBA
8 Strong, J. 1996. The exhaustive concordance of the Bible : Showing every word of the test of the common English version of the canonical books, and every occurence of each word in regular order. (electronic ed.) . Woodside Bible Fellowship.: Ontario
9 Strong, J. 1996
10Wiersbe, W. W. 1996, c1989. *The Bible exposition commentary*. "An exposition of the New Testament comprising the entire 'BE' series"--Jkt. Victor Books: Wheaton, Ill.
11 Vine, W.E., Vine's Complete Expository Dictionary, "Hold Fast, " Thomas Nelson, 1976, pg.306.
12 James Swanson, Dictionary of Biblical Languages with Semantic Domains: Greek (New Testament) (Oak Harbor: Logos Research Systems, Inc., 1997).
13 ibid
14 Strong, J. 1996. The exhaustive concordance of the Bible : Showing every word of the test of the common English version of the canonical books, and every occurence of each word in regular order. (electronic ed.) . Woodside Bible Fellowship.: Ontario
15 James Swanson, Dictionary of Biblical Languages with Semantic Domains: Greek (New Testament) (Oak Harbor: Logos Research Systems, Inc., 1997).
16 Dictionary, "Rebellion", Dictionary.com LLC 2019, https://www.dictionary.com/browse/rebellion, March 13, 2019.
17James Swanson, Dictionary of Biblical Languages with Semantic Domains: Greek (New Testament) (Oak Harbor: Logos Research Systems, Inc., 1997).
18Strong, J. 1996. *The exhaustive concordance of the Bible*
19Strong, J. 1996.
1 Stacy Liberator, The Daily Mail.com, Sept. 15, 2016, http://www.dailymail.co.uk/sciencetech/article-3789923/Mysterious-onyx-stone-thought-ancient-prophetic-gem-breastplate-High-Priest-Jerusalem.html June 6, 2018
2 Crownover, Rose, Precious Stones of the Bible, "Onyx" Stones of the Bible 2007-2012, http://www.preciousstonesofthebible.com/stonegallery.html, Nov. 2, 2018

³ Crownover, Rose, Stones of the Bible, "Onyx," Color Symbolism, 2007-2012
http://www.preciousstonesofthebible.com/colorsymbolism.html, Nov. 2, 2018

⁴ Strong, J. 1996. The exhaustive concordance of the Bible : Showing every word of the test of the common English version of the canonical books, and every occurrence of each word in regular order. (electronic ed.) . Woodside Bible Fellowship.: Ontario

⁵ Herchel, Abraham Joshua. *God in Search of Man, A Philosophy of Judaism*. New York. Farrar, Straus and Giroux, Paperback ed. 1976, 34.

⁶ James Swanson, Dictionary of Biblical Languages with Semantic Domains: Greek (New Testament) (Oak Harbor: Logos Research Systems, Inc., 1997).

⁷ Strong, J. 1996. The exhaustive concordance of the Bible : Showing every word of the test of the common English version of the canonical books, and every occurrence of each word in regular order. (electronic ed.) . Woodside Bible Fellowship.: Ontario

⁸ James Swanson, Dictionary of Biblical Languages with Semantic Domains : Hebrew (Old Testament) (Oak Harbor: Logos Research Systems, Inc., 1997).

⁹ Ibid

¹⁰ John J. Parsons, Hebrew4Christians, "The Just Shall Live by Faith",
https://www.hebrew4christians.com/Meditations/By_Faith/by_faith.html, Aug.10, 2020

¹¹ Ibid

¹² James Swanson, Dictionary of Biblical Languages with Semantic Domains: Greek (New Testament) (Oak Harbor: Logos Research Systems, Inc., 1997).

¹³ James Swanson, Dictionary of Biblical Languages with Semantic Domains: Greek (New Testament) (Oak Harbor: Logos Research Systems, Inc., 1997).

¹⁴ Dictionary.com, "Pierce", https://www.dictionary.com/browse/pierce, Aug. 10, 2020

Chapter 5

¹ https://en.wikipedia.org/wiki/Engagement_ring_of_Lady_Diana_Spencer

² Jone, Bob and Davis, Keith, Sapphire Church.org, https://www.sapphirechurch.org/the-significance-of-sapphire June 2018

³ Crownover, Rose, "Sapphire" Stones of the Bible 2007-2012, Sept, 2018http://www.preciousstonesofthebible.com/colorsymbolism.html

⁴Strong, J. 1996. *The exhaustive concordance of the Bible: Showing every word of the test of the common English version of the canonical books, and every occurrence of each word in regular order.* (electronic ed.) . Woodside Bible Fellowship.: Ontario

⁵ Wiersbe, W. W. 1996, c1989. The Bible exposition commentary

Chapter 6

¹ http://www.opalsdownunder.com.au/learn-about-opals/introductory/famous-opals

²http://www.allhebrewnames.com/hebnames/en/name_details.seam?nameID=1755

³ The Geological Institute of America, Inc. "Overview" Opal, 2002-2018, April 5, 2018
https://www.gia.edu/opal

⁴ Crownover, Rose, Precious Stones of the Bible, "Opal" Stones of the Bible 2007-2012, April 5, 2018http://www.preciousstonesofthebible.com/stonegallery.html

⁵ Wiersbe, W. W. 1996, c1989. The Bible exposition commentary. "An exposition of the New Testament comprising the entire 'BE' series"--Jkt. Victor Books: Wheaton, Ill.

⁶ James Swanson, Dictionary of Biblical Languages with Semantic Domains: Greek (New Testament) (Oak Harbor: Logos Research Systems, Inc., 1997).

⁷ Strong, J. 1996. The exhaustive concordance of the Bible : Showing every word of the test of the common English version of the canonical books, and every occurrence of each word in regular order. (electronic ed.) . Woodside Bible Fellowship.: Ontario

⁸ Strong, J. 1996

⁹ Dictionary.com, 2019. "Idioms" https://www.dictionary.com/browse/deny?s=t Jan. 23, 2019
¹⁰ Google, 2019
https://www.google.com/search?source=hp&ei=7MhJXO2DHY7usQWYo6GQAg&q=just+meaning&btnK=Google+Search&oq=just+meaning&gs_l=psy-ab.3..0l10.627.7489..15791...0.0..0.239.2269.0j10j3......0....1..gws-wiz.....0..35i39j0i131.HHAzuj5WP5A

Chapter 7

¹ https://www.si.edu/spotlight/hope-diamond
² http://www.pbs.org/treasuresoftheworld/a_nav/hope_nav/main_hopfrm.
³ Swanson, J. (1997). *Dictionary of Biblical Languages with Semantic Domains : Hebrew (Old Testament)* (electronic ed.). Oak Harbor: Logos Research Systems, Inc.
⁴ Arthur, Kay, *To Know Him by Name*, Multnomah Books, 1995. Pages 61 and 64.
⁵ Elisabeth Rosenthal and Andrew Martin, New York Times, World, 2008, https://www.nytimes.com/2008/06/04/news/04iht-04food.13446176.html, July 29, 2019.
⁶ Michael S. Heiser and Vincent M. Setterholm, Glossary of Morpho-Syntactic Database Terminology (Lexham Press, 2013; 2013).
⁷ James Swanson, Dictionary of Biblical Languages with Semantic Domains: Greek (New Testament) (Oak Harbor: Logos Research Systems, Inc., 1997).
⁸ Stern, David H., The New Jewish Commentary, Jewish New Testament Publications, 1992, pg. 680
⁹ James Swanson, Dictionary of Biblical Languages with Semantic Domains: Greek (New Testament) (Oak Harbor: Logos Research Systems, Inc., 1997).
¹⁰ Ibid
¹¹ Collins, "Definition of hetero", https://www.collinsdictionary.com/us/dictionary/english/hetero, Aug. 11, 2020
¹² Swanson, J. (1997). *Dictionary of Biblical Languages with Semantic Domains: Greek (New Testament)* (electronic ed.). Oak Harbor: Logos Research Systems, Inc.
¹³ Bible Sense Lexicon, Logos Bible Software, Oct. 3, 2018
¹⁴ Ibid, April 2018
¹⁵ Ibid, April 2018
¹⁶Strong, J. 1996. *The exhaustive concordance of the Bible : Showing every word of the test of the common English version of the canonical books, and every occurrence of each word in regular order.* (electronic ed.) . Woodside Bible Fellowship.: Ontario
¹⁷ Swanson, J. (1997). *Dictionary of Biblical Languages with Semantic Domains: Greek (New Testament)* (electronic ed.). Oak Harbor: Logos Research Systems, Inc.
¹⁸ Swanson, J. (1997). *Dictionary of Biblical Languages with Semantic Domains: Greek (New Testament)* (electronic ed.). Oak Harbor: Logos Research Systems, Inc.
¹⁹ Baker & Baker Jewelers, "Gemstone Guide - Gemstone Glossary", Heart Cut, 2018, April 23, 2018 http://www.bakernbaker.com/Component/Education/Gemstone_Guide/Gemstone_Glossary

Chapter 8

¹ https://www.truefacet.com/guide/lustrous-luxurious-worlds-expensive-pearls/
² https://en.wikipedia.org/wiki/Nacre
³ http://www.preciousstonesofthebible.com/colorsymbolism.html
⁴ James Swanson, Dictionary of Biblical Languages with Semantic Domains: Greek (New Testament) (Oak Harbor: Logos Research Systems, Inc., 1997).
⁵ Ibid
⁶ Eli Lizorkin-Eyzenberg, *The Jewish Gospel of John*, (Tel Mond, Israel: Israel Study Center, 2015) xi-xiii
⁷ James Swanson, Dictionary of Biblical Languages with Semantic Domains: Greek (New Testament) (Oak Harbor: Logos Research Systems, Inc., 1997). Strong's #4639
⁸ http://www.wildbranch.org/teachings/lessons/lesson33.html

⁹http://lexiconcordance.com/hebrew/1129.html
¹⁰ Lovik, Craig John, Video "Tabernacle" (parts 1, 2, 3, and 4), July 3, 2018, https://www.youtube.com/watch?time_continue=6&v=Lp_MvUIoQBA
¹¹ The Meaning of Passover, 2018, https://chosenpeople.com/site/the-meaning-of-passover/
¹² Mackie, Timothy, The Bible Project, "What is the Shema?", July 10, 2018, https://thebibleproject.com/blog/what-is-the-shema/.
¹³Strong, J. 1996. The exhaustive concordance of the Bible #854/DBL Greek, Logos Bible Software, July 11, 2018.

Chapter 9

¹ Cohen, Howard, The Jeweler Blog, "23-Carat Carmen Lúcia Ruby Is One of the World's Most Extraordinary Examples of July's Birthstone," July 12, 2018, https://thejewelerblog.wordpress.com/2017/07/10/23-carat-carmen-lucia-ruby-is-one-of-the-worldd-most-extraordinary-examples-of-julys-birthstone/.
² Gemological Institute of America Inc., "Ruby Quality Factors", 2002-2018, https://www.gia.edu/ruby-quality-factor.
³ Stones of the Bible, "Color Symbolism," 2007, http://www.preciousstonesofthebible.com/colorsymbolism.html.
⁴ Google, Dictionary, Worship, https://www.google.com/search?rlz=1C1CAFA_enUS630US711&q=Dictionary#dobs=worship, Aug. 10, 2018.
⁵ Scott, Brad, The Tabernacle, "The Ark", published by Wildbranch Ministry, accessed Aug. 15, 2018, http://www.wildbranch.org/teachings/lessons/lesson33.html
⁶ Donald Guthrie, *Hebrews: An Introduction and Commentary*, vol. 15, Tyndale New Testament Commentaries (Downers Grove, IL: InterVarsity Press, 1983), 185.
⁷ Donald Guthrie, Hebrews: An Introduction and Commentary, vol. 15, Tyndale New Testament Commentaries (Downers Grove, IL: InterVarsity Press, 1983), 189–190.
⁸Google, Dictionary, Aug. 28, 2018 https://www.google.com/search?q=redemption+definition&rlz=1C1CAFA_enUS630US711&oq=redemption&aqs=chrome.3.69i57j0l5.3328j0j7&sourceid=chrome&ie=UTF-8
⁹Wiersbe, W. W. 1996, c1989. The Bible exposition commentary. "An exposition of the New Testament comprising the entire 'BE' series"--Jkt. Victor Books: Wheaton, Ill. Aug. 31, 2018.
¹⁰ Jamieson, R., Fausset, A. R., Fausset, A. R., Brown, D., & Brown, D. 1997. A commentary, critical and explanatory, on the Old and New Testaments. On spine: Critical and explanatory commentary. Logos Research Systems, Inc.: Oak Harbor, WA Sept. 6, 2018
¹¹ Wiersbe, W. W. 1996, c1989. The Bible exposition commentary. "An exposition of the New Testament comprising the entire 'BE' series"--Jkt. Victor Books: Wheaton, Ill. Sept. 6, 2018
¹² Young, Brad H., *Jesus, the Jewish Theologian*, (Grand Rapids: Baker Publishing Group, 1995), 243-252

Chapter 10

¹ The Jewelry Editor, "L'Incomparable diamond necklace,"http://www.thejewelleryeditor.com/shop/product/incomparable-diamond-necklace/, Aug. 14, 2019.
² Cathaway, Tony, Arpege Diamonds, Naturally Colored Diamond Blog, "The Most Famous Yellow Diamonds in the World," June 6, 2016, https://blog.arpegediamonds.com/the-most-famous-yellow-diamonds-in-the-world, Aug. 14, 2019.
³ Cathaway, Tony, Arpege Diamonds, Naturally Colored Diamond Blog, "The Most Famous Yellow Diamonds in the World," June 6, 2016, https://blog.arpegediamonds.com/the-most-famous-yellow-diamonds-in-the-world, Aug. 14, 2019.
⁴ Dictionary.com, "Incomparable", COLLINS ENGLISH DICTIONARY - COMPLETE & UNABRIDGED 2012 DIGITAL EDITION, https://www.dictionary.com/browse/incomparable, Aug. 14, 2019.
⁵ Crownover, Rose, Precious Stones of the Bible, "Stones of the Bible", 2007-2012, http://www.preciousstonesofthebible.com/colorsymbolism.html, Sept. 27, 2018

[6] James Swanson, Dictionary of Biblical Languages with Semantic Domains: Greek (New Testament) (Oak Harbor: Logos Research Systems, Inc., 1997).

[7] Ibid

[8] Inc Merriam-Webster, Merriam-Webster's Collegiate Dictionary. (Springfield, MA: Merriam-Webster, Inc., 2003).

[9] James Swanson, Dictionary of Biblical Languages with Semantic Domains: Greek (New Testament) (Oak Harbor: Logos Research Systems, Inc., 1997).

[10] Dwight M. Pratt, "Apostasy", Quick Reference Dictionary, Bible Study Tools, https://www.biblestudytools.com/dictionary/apostasy-apostate/ Oct. 8, 2018

[11] James Swanson, Dictionary of Biblical Languages with Semantic Domains: Greek (New Testament) (Oak Harbor: Logos Research Systems, Inc., 1997).

[12] James Swanson, Dictionary of Biblical Languages with Semantic Domains: Greek (New Testament) (Oak Harbor: Logos Research Systems, Inc., 1997).

[13] Ibid

[14] James Swanson, Dictionary of Biblical Languages with Semantic Domains: Greek (New Testament) (Oak Harbor: Logos Research Systems, Inc., 1997).

[15] Wiersbe, W. W. 1996, c1989. The Bible exposition commentary. "An exposition of the New Testament comprising the entire 'BE' series"--Jkt. Victor Books: Wheaton, Ill.

Chapter 11

[1] Jewels For Me, "Lapis Meaning, Powers and History", 2002, https://www.jewelsforme.com/gem_and_jewelry_library/lapis, Oct. 10, 2018

[2] Roderick Conway Morris, New York Times, "Lapis Lazuli and the History of 'the Most Perfect' Color," Aug. 18, 2015, https://www.nytimes.com/2015/08/19/arts/international/lapis-lazuli-and-the-history-of-the-most-perfect-color.html

[3] Jewels For Me, "Lapis Meaning, Powers and History", 2002, https://www.jewelsforme.com/gem_and_jewelry_library/lapis, Oct. 10, 2018

[4] Crownover, Rose, Precious Stones of the Bible, "Stones of the Bible", 2007-2012, http://www.preciousstonesofthebible.com/colorsymbolism.html, Oct. 10, 2018

[5] Oswald Chambers Quotes. BrainyQuote.com, BrainyMedia Inc, 2019. https://www.brainyquote.com/quotes/oswald_chambers_386812, accessed February 4, 2019.

[6] Blue Letter Bible, Lexicon, Strongs #G5258, 2019 https://www.blueletterbible.org/lang/lexicon/lexicon.cfm?Strongs=G5259, Jan. 23, 2019

[7] Blue Letter Bible, Lexicon, Strongs # G2476, 2019, https://www.blueletterbible.org/lang/lexicon/lexicon.cfm?Strongs=G2476, Jan. 23, 2019

[8] James Swanson, Dictionary of Biblical Languages with Semantic Domains: Greek (New Testament) (Oak Harbor: Logos Research Systems, Inc., 1997). Strong's #5287

[9] Bible Hub, Strongs #1650. 2004-2018. https://biblehub.com/greek/1650.htm, Jan. 24, 2019

[10] James Swanson, Dictionary of Biblical Languages with Semantic Domains: Greek (New Testament) (Oak Harbor: Logos Research Systems, Inc., 1997). Feb. 5, 2019

[11] Merriam-Webster, Incorporated, "Definition of Foundation", https://www.merriam-webster.com/dictionary/foundation, Feb. 5, 2019.

[12] Wikipedia, the Free Encyclopedia, "Cornerstone", 19 October 2018, https://en.wikipedia.org/wiki/Cornerstone, Feb. 5, 2019

[13] James Swanson, 1997.

[14] Chambers, Oswald, My Upmost for His Highest, Aug. 29th, Dodd Mead and Company, Inc. 1935.

Chapter 12

[1] Novel Collection, Natural Fancy Color Specialist, "Fancy Color Diamonds Grading", 2017, http://novel-collection.com/fancy-color-diamonds-grading/, Aug. 14, 2019.

2 Dinelli, Pinot C, ICON Jewels, "The Leonardo Da Vinci Of Diamonds," Nov. 23, 2018,https://www.iconjewelsusa.com/single-post/2018/11/23/The-Leonardo-Da-Vinci-Of-Diamonds--, Aug. 14, 2019.

3 Weisberger, Mindy, Live Science, "Giant 'Pink Legacy' Diamond Fetches Over $44 Million at Auction," Nov. 2018 https://www.livescience.com/64080-pink-legacy-diamond-auction.html, Aug. 2019.

4 Ibid

5 Crownover, Rose, Precious Stones of the Bible, "Stones of the Bible", 2007-2012, http://www.preciousstonesofthebible.com/colorsymbolism.html, Aug. 2019

6 Amato, Scott, Livestrong.com, "The Physical Difference Between Long Distance Runners & Sprinters", June 13, 2019, https://www.livestrong.com/article/550102-the-physical-difference-between-long-distance-runners-sprinters/.

7 Ibid

8 James Swanson, Dictionary of Biblical Languages with Semantic Domains: Greek (New Testament) (Oak Harbor: Logos Research Systems, Inc., 1997).

9 Ibid

10 Ibid

11 Allen, David L., The New American Commentary, Hebrews, B & H Publishing, 2010, pg. 581, June 28, 2019.

12 Dictionary.com, LLC, "Lame", 2019, https://www.dictionary.com/browse/lame, July 8, 2019.

13 Strong, J. 1996. The exhaustive concordance of the Bible : Showing every word of the test of the common English version of the canonical books, and every occurrence of each word in regular order. (electronic ed.) . Woodside Bible Fellowship.: Ontario

14 James Swanson, Dictionary of Biblical Languages with Semantic Domains: Greek (New Testament) (Oak Harbor: Logos Research Systems, Inc., 1997).to pollute or stain.

15 Ibid

16 Ibid

17 Ibid

18 Blue Letter Bible, Lexicon :: Strong's G2618 – katakaiō, 2019, https://www.blueletterbible.org/lang/lexicon/lexicon.cfm?Strongs=G2618&t=NLT, July 12, 2019

19 James Swanson, Dictionary of Biblical Languages with Semantic Domains: Greek (New Testament) (Oak Harbor: Logos Research Systems, Inc., 1997).to pollute or stain.

Chapter 13

1 GIA, "Famous Birthstones: Garnet – The Antique Pyrope Hair Comb," Aug. 2019, https://4cs.gia.edu/en-us/blog/famous-gemstones-pyrope-garnet/

2 Ibid

3 Phoebe Shang, GG, "International Gem Society," Garnet Symbolism, 2019https://www.gemsociety.org/article/garnet-symbolism-legends/

4 Stones of the Bible, "Color Symbolism," 2007, http://www.preciousstonesofthebible.com/colorsymbolism.html.

5 James Swanson, Dictionary of Biblical Languages with Semantic Domains: Greek (New Testament) (Oak Harbor: Logos Research Systems, Inc., 1997). Strong's #430

6 Zondervan Academic, "Who Wrote the Book of Hebrews?," HarperCollins Publishers, 2019, https://zondervanacademic.com/blog/who-wrote-the-book-of-hebrews, Nov. 15, 2019.

7 Sar Shalom - Messianic Jewish Community, "Divorce & Re-Marriage," Sept. 14, 2016https://rabbiyeshua.com/item/49-divorce-remarriage, Oct. 14, 2019.

8 Ibid

9 Young, Brad H., Jesus the Jewish Theologian, Baker Academic, 1995, pg. 115.

10 James Swanson, Dictionary of Biblical Languages with Semantic Domains: Greek (New Testament) (Oak Harbor: Logos Research Systems, Inc., 1997).

11 Zoran Strajin, Chapel of Adam, the Church of the Holy Sepulchre – Jerusalem, Nov. 18, 2010, https://www.360cities.net/image/chapel-of-adam-the-church-of-the-holy-sepulchre-jerusalem

[12] Rev Aaron Eime is the deacon of Christ Church in the Old City of Jerusalem, the first Protestant Church in the Middle East. Aaron studied at the Hebrew University in the Master's Program with the focus towards Early Jewish and Christian Interpretation of Bible. He is a dedicated Bible teacher exploring the Hebraic Roots of the Christian Faith. He has taught internationally in many countries including Europe, North America, Hong Kong and China. Aaron is the Director of Research and Education at Christ Church. He lives in Jerusalem with his wife and 3 children.

[13] Ibid

[14] James Swanson, Dictionary of Biblical Languages with Semantic Domains: Greek (New Testament) (Oak Harbor: Logos Research Systems, Inc., 1997).

[15] CBN News, "American Hostage Kayla Mueller Remembered for Defending Her Faith before ISIS,"https://www1.cbn.com/cbnnews/us/2016/august/american-hostage-kayla-mueller-remembered-for-defending-her-faith-before-isis, Nov. 1, 2019.

[16] James Swanson, Dictionary of Biblical Languages with Semantic Domains: Greek (New Testament) (Oak Harbor: Logos Research Systems, Inc., 1997).

CPSIA information can be obtained
at www.ICGtesting.com
Printed in the USA
BVHW010551301120
594467BV00010B/246